# The Life in the Spirit Seminars Team Manual

## Catholic Edition

**DEVELOPED BY THE WORD OF GOD
ANN ARBOR, MICHIGAN**

**SERVANT BOOKS
ANN ARBOR, MICHIGAN**

1st Edition, January 1971          25,000
2nd Edition, January 1972          25,000
3rd Edition, September 1973        80,000
Catholic Edition, January 1979


Imprimatur:    Leo A. Pursley, D.D.
               Bishop of Fort Wayne-South Bend

Published by:
  Servant Books
  Box 8617
  Ann Arbor, Michigan 48107




Scripture taken from the Revised Standard Version.
Used with permission.

ISBN 0-89283-065-4

# The Life in the Spirit Seminars Team Manual

"To the thirsty I will give water without price from the fountain of the water of life... Let him who is thirsty come, let him who desires take the water of life without price." (Rev. 21:6, 22:17)

# Contents

# Contents

# INTRODUCTION

The Life in the Spirit Seminars have been very widely used throughout the world. They have been translated into many languages and used by many types of groups, both ecumenical groups and church-related groups of a variety of backgrounds. The seminars have been very commonly used by Catholic groups in the context of renewal in the Roman Catholic Church, and this use has produced a demand for a Catholic version. The original edition said, "adaptations of the seminars can certainly be made." Many Catholic groups have already made them for their own situation and have sent copies of their adaptations. The following version has profited a great deal from some of these revisions.

The original Life in the Spirit Seminars was designed for a very evangelistic situation. They were developed in a community which evangelized people at home, at work, in social situations and not primarily in church contexts. Those who came to the seminars were in a great variety of spiritual conditions ranging from active church-goers, to nominal church-goers, to people who had given up the practice of Christianity, to unbelievers. The seminars were designed as a tool to be able to reach a wide range of such people. Many others, however, used the seminars in situations that could best be described as church-renewal situations. The seminars were given in parish or other church contexts, and they were used primarily for people who already had a clear identification with a particular church to bring those church members to a fuller experience of life in the Spirit. The seminars have been used especially commonly in this way by Catholics.

This edition of the seminars has such situations in mind. It is designed to be used by groups that are identified as being Catholic or that mainly draw Catholics in search of renewal. It can also be used as an evangelistic tool where all the people who would come are either Catholic or come from Catholic backgrounds (as in a Catholic country or neighborhood, for instance). Where the group that is sponsoring the seminars is ecumenical or nondenominational or where the group is directly evangelizing people of mixed church background, we would recommend using the revised edition. Orthodox and some Episcopalian and Lutheran groups may find that the Catholic edition could also be used by them with some adaptation.

Even in situations designed to take good Catholics and to bring them to a deeper life in the Spirit, however, the Life in the Spirit Seminars have a primarily evangelistic character. They are designed to take the basic message of Christianity and to proclaim it anew so that those who hear it can make a renewed commitment to the Lord in a way which will allow them to receive a fuller experience of the work of the Spirit in their lives. They are not designed as catechetics or as a course in adult education or as a theological update on the charismatic renewal. Experience indicates that those who

2

wish to adapt the seminar for Catholic use often inadvertently weaken or obscure the evangelistic thrust of the seminars, and they consequently reduce its power and effectiveness as an instrument for bringing people into a deeper experience of the work of the Holy Spirit.

Therefore, those who use the seminars should keep three points in mind: (1) the basic presentation of the gospel (especially as found in the second seminar) should not be eliminated or attenuated. It should be stated clearly, simply, and with conviction. Many Catholics need to hear the gospel again in order to respond with an authentic and deeper commitment to Christ; (2) the basic teaching about what the Lord is willing to do for all who come to him can be stated in a simple enough way to by-pass all dogmatic or theological questions and reach directly to a person's heart; and (3) serious theological issues are usually best taken care of outside the seminars and not in them.

The Catholic edition of the seminars aims to integrate the message of the seminars more clearly into the Catholic life of the participants. This has meant explicitly considering the sacraments and the liturgical life of the church, as well as situating the new life more clearly in the context of the life of the Catholic Church. Comments have also been added to help team members be clearer on the Catholic perspective on the theological questions raised by the seminars.

The Second Vatican Council called for the spiritual renewal of the spiritual life of the Catholic people. It is hoped that the Life in the Spirit Seminars can be an instrument for that spiritual renewal and for the answering of the prayer which Pope John asked us to pray for the Council: "Renew in our day, O Lord, your wonders as in a new Pentecost."

March 1978

# PART ONE

# THE WORK
# OF THE TEAM

In his first letter to the Corinthians, Paul the apostle wrote:

"According to the commission of God given to me, like a skilled master builder I laid a foundation, and another man is building upon it. Let each man take care how he builds upon it." (1 Cor. 3:10)

Paul thought of himself as a craftsman, a skilled worker in the service of the Lord. In order to serve the Lord as an apostle, he had to acquire certain skills; he had to learn to work carefully. He was a man whom the Spirit led with specific guidance and instructions, he experienced the Lord working signs and wonders through him, but still he needed to learn a skill. He had to learn to build well in order to build up God's temple, the Christian community in Corinth.

How does the Lord train his master craftsmen, those whom he appoints to the work of building his kingdom? How can they acquire the skills and abilities they need? In the thirty-fifth chapter of Exodus, Moses told the people of Israel how the Lord had prepared craftsmen to work on his sanctuary:

"See, the Lord has called by name Bezalel the son of Uri, son of Hur, of the tribe of Judah; and he has filled him with the Spirit of God, with ability, with intelligence, with knowledge, and with all craftsmanship, to devise artistic designs, to work in gold and silver and bronze, in cutting stones for setting, and in carving wood, for work in every skilled craft. And he has inspired him to teach, both him and Oholiab. He has filled them with ability to do every sort of work done by a craftsman or by a designer, or by an embroiderer in blue and purple and scarlet stuff and fine twined linen, or by a weaver—by any sort of workman or skilled designer. Bezalel and Oholiab and every able man in whom the Lord has put ability and intelligence to know how to do any work in the construction of the sanctuary, shall work in accordance with all that the Lord has commanded." (Ex 35:30-36:1)

When the Lord chose craftsmen to build his sanctuary, he filled them with the Holy Spirit, and the Holy Spirit brought to them the ability and understanding they needed to build well. Their skill was a gift of the Holy Spirit, their ability to teach others was inspired by the Lord. Even though the Lord had given the Israelites specific and minutely detailed instructions for the design of the tabernacle, they needed to be given the ability and craftsmanship by the Holy Spirit to execute those designs properly.

The Lord is working to build his church today in the

same way that he worked to build his tabernacle among the people of Israel, or to build the Christian community at Corinth. He has called us to be craftsmen, to be builders in his plan. And the same Holy Spirit that brought ability and understanding to the craftsmen for the tabernacle will work in us to give us the ability and understanding and skill we need to build up the people of God. The Holy Spirit wants to make us skillful builders.

As we begin to work in the Life in the Spirit Seminars, we have to be prepared to acquire that spiritual craftsmanship. We have to turn to the Lord and let the Holy Spirit give us the wisdom and ability we need to build well. We cannot be careless and negligent, expecting the Lord to fill in for our neglect, saying, "The Lord will take care of everything." The Lord will take care of our seminars, and we can count on him to do things that are far beyond our powers. But one of the most powerful ways that the Lord uses to care for things is to give us the spiritual gifts that will make us skillful in leading people to him. Prophecy, tongues, healing, and miracles are spiritual gifts, but so are wisdom and understanding. Giving us skill is one of the main ways the Lord wants to take care of everything.

If someone entrusted us with a million dollars, we would be very, very careful with it. We would probably be awed at the amount that was in our charge. And yet each person the Lord puts in our care is of far more value to him than a million dollars. He is entrusting to us men and women who will live eternally, men and women for whom he died. He wants us to serve them with even more reverence and care than we would have for a million dollars.

# THE SEMINARS

In his great discourse at the Last Supper, Jesus made a promise to his disciples:

"I will pray the Father and he will give you another Counselor, to be with you forever, even the Spirit of Truth, whom the world cannot receive because it neither sees him nor knows him; you know him, for he dwells with you and will be in you."     (Jn 14:16-17)

Jesus knew that when he was no longer on earth, his disciples would not be able to live the kind of life he had called them to by their own strength and ability. He knew that Christians would need a supernatural source of strength, that they would need the strength and power of God himself. So he promised to his disciples the very Spirit of

God, and on Pentecost that Spirit came down upon them, to remain with the Christian people forever. The lives of the disciples were radically transformed by the Holy Spirit: they were able to preach the Gospel of Jesus in boldness and power, their words were accompanied by signs and wonders, they drew together to live in new communities, united in one mind and one heart.

Today Christians of all denominations are rediscovering the power that Jesus gives his people through the Holy Spirit. They are discovering the power to live together in love and peace, to heal the sick and comfort the afflicted, and to worship God with new and abundant praise. Above all, they are discovering a deeper and more personal relationship with Jesus Christ as their very own Lord and Savior. The power of the Holy Spirit has made such a vital and tangible change in their lives that more and more people can see that power at work and begin to desire this new life for themselves. Everywhere, people are coming alive to the new life in the Spirit, and they want to find out more about that life, they want to discover a new relationship with Jesus.

The Life in the Spirit Seminars are designed as an introduction to a life lived in the power of the Holy Spirit. They provide an opportunity for people to find out more about that life, and to be helped in taking the first steps of a new relationship with the Lord. For those who are not Christians at all, they can serve as an introduction to Christianity and a time to make a first commitment to Jesus Christ. For those who are already Christians, they offer help in finding a fuller release of the Holy Spirit to live a deeper Christian life.

The seminars are a series of talks and discussions which take place over a period of seven weeks. In the fifth week of the seminar, there is an opportunity for people to be prayed with to be baptized in the Holy Spirit. The four weeks

9

before that time are devoted to an explanation of the basic Christian message of salvation and of what it means to be baptized in the Spirit. During the final two weeks, the teaching is oriented towards further growth in the life of the Spirit.

But more than a series of courses or lectures, the Life in the Spirit Seminars are a chance for Christians who have found a fuller life in the Holy Spirit to come together with people who want to know more about that life, to share with them, and to help them take the first steps of a new life themselves. For this reason, the team that presents the seminars is one of their most important elements. To provide the right kind of contact for the people taking the seminars, there should be one team member for every three or four new people.

The Life in the Spirit Seminars have a very limited goal. They are designed to be only the beginning, only the first step in a completely new way of life. For people to continue to grow and develop in this new life they need to come together with others who are living this same way to receive support and further teaching. For this reason, the seminars should be presented in the context of a Christian community or prayer group where people are already living the life in the Spirit together. People completing the seminars should be brought into the life of these groups where they can receive the guidance and support they will need to go on with their new life.

## GOAL

The goal of the Life in the Spirit Seminars is very limited. They are designed to help people find a new and fuller and better life as Christians by laying or strengthening the foundation of a truly Christian life. "No other foundation can anyone lay than that which is laid, which is

Jesus Christ." (I Cor 3:11). The seminars, then, are concerned with the most basic part of Christian life: establishing a person in Christ. To accomplish that goal, there are four things the Life in the Spirit Seminars try to do.

## LIFE IN THE SPIRIT SEMINARS TRY :

**1** to help those who come to the seminars establish or re-establish or deepen *a personal relationship with Christ;*

**2** to help those who come to the seminars to yield to *the action of the Holy Spirit in their lives* so that they can begin to experience his presence and can begin to experience him working in them and through them;

**3** to help those who come to the seminars be joined to Christ more fully by becoming part of *a community* or a group of Christians with whom they can share their Christian life and from whom they can receive support in that life;

**4** to help them begin to make use of effective *means of growth* in their relationship with Christ.

There are many things that people need besides these, but it is better for us to do what we can do well than to take on too many things and have none of them achieve their goal.

If done well, the Life in the Spirit Seminars will bring people to the point where they want to go on in the Christian life. They have made the basic commitment, they have experienced God and the effects of faith, they have a hunger for the things of the Spirit. They need more help if they are to go further, but they should be ready to go further.

# PROGRESSION

The Life in the Spirit Seminars have a simple progression that leads towards and away from the fifth week. In the first four weeks, the people in the seminars are prepared to turn to the Lord in a deeper way and establish a more effective relationship with him. In the fifth week they are led to make a commitment to Christ and they are prayed with to be baptized in the Spirit. In the last two weeks, they are helped to enter into a process of growth in the new relationship they now have with the Lord.

**WEEK 1**     In the first seminar, everyone is new. Some need motivation to make the decision to stay. All need an orientation toward the seminars that will prepare them to make use of the seminars more fruitfully. The first seminar is mainly introductory. The presentation talks in a simple way about God's love and his desire to have a personal relationship with us. Most of the presentation explains the seminar program.

**WEEK 2**     The second seminar focuses on the need of people to see how momentous a thing they are getting themselves into. Being a committed Christian, being baptized in the Spirit, involves a reorientation of life that is significantly different from the way the ordinary modern man thinks—it is, in fact, a revolution in outlook on the world. The presentation explains the basic gospel message in a way that allows the people in the seminar to see how great the salvation is that is being offered to them and how great a difference there is between living under the rule of Christ and the rule of the world.

**WEEK 3**

The third seminar centers on the promise of new life. It helps the people taking the seminar realize the goodness of the gift being offered to them. This is the seminar in which the explanation is given about what it means to be baptized in the Spirit.

**WEEK 4**

The fourth seminar is the week of preparation for commitment to Christ and for being baptized in the Spirit. This is the week in which the steps to begin the Christian life (or to reestablish or deepen the Christian life) are explained. This is the week in which the needed reorientation of a person's life should be accomplished. The presentation explains how to turn to the Lord (repentance and faith) and what is involved in being baptized in the Spirit. In the personal contact with the discussion leader, the people in the seminar can work out any problems and receive personal help.

---

**WEEK 5**    The fifth seminar is the seminar in which people are led to a commitment to Christ and are prayed with to be baptized in the Spirit and to receive the gift of tongues. The whole seminar is set aside for making the commitment to Christ and for prayer for release of the Spirit.

---

**WEEK 6**    The sixth seminar is the first session dedicated to going on in the Christian life. In it people should begin to make the decision and changes of life necessary to preserve the new life they have begun to experience. The focus of the presentation this week is on personal prayer time and community.

---

**WEEK 7**    The seventh seminar is the final session. It is oriented toward helping people to go on with the life in the Spirit, especially toward helping them take the concrete steps they need to take to be part of a particular community or prayer group. The presentation centers on the work of the Holy Spirit changing us, the trials and difficulties which come up, and the way of entering into the life of the community or prayer group.

The first four weeks of the seminars center on the basic Christian message. They are an explanation of the four basic truths of Christianity that were presented in the explanation session and are designed to lead a person to make a deeper commitment to Christ. The last two weeks are an instruction in how to go on from that new commitment. They are "follow-up" instructions and are designed to make clear the need for more to happen in people's lives for the new beginning to be effective in a new life.

# THE TEAM

Jesus reaches out to men through the members of his body. The new life he wants to give he offers through men and women in whom his Spirit lives. More than anything else, the Life in the Spirit Seminars are Christians who have been given a fuller life in the Spirit coming together to share that gift with others who have not yet found it.

The team members are above all witnesses. They are men and women who are living the life of the Spirit and who can witness to its reality and effectiveness for themselves. In order for them to be witnesses, they have to be able to speak the truth in a simple way. Men should not only see the life in them but also learn about it from them.

Jesus is the one who baptizes in the Holy Spirit. The team are members of his body through whom he works. He has entrusted his Spirit to them so that as they allow his Spirit to speak and act through them, others can meet him in a new way.

Paul spoke to Timothy about how he should be a servant of the Lord. Paul's exhortation to Timothy is also an exhortation to those who work on Life in the Spirit teams:

"Let no one despise your youth, but set the believers an example in speech and conduct, in love, in faith, in purity. . . Take heed to yourselves and to your teaching; hold to that, for by so doing you will save both yourself and your hearers." (I Tim 4:12, 16)

# THE TEAM MEMBER

Paul told Timothy, "What you have heard from me before many witnesses entrust to faithful men who will be able to teach others also" (II Tim 2:2). Paul knew that he could not reach everyone in the world by himself. The gifts and the abilities he had, had to be imparted to others, so that the work of Christ could increase throughout the whole world. Nor could Timothy even care for the needs of the Christian community at Ephesus. A one-man pastoral work is inadequate for what the Lord wants to do.

When Paul instructed Timothy to choose men to share in the work, he picked out two characteristics as being essential: **faithfulness** and **ability**. The person had to be faithful, that is, he had to be reliable. He had to be the kind of person that could be counted on. If someone would be entrusted to him, he would do his best to care for the person who was his responsibility. He also had to have ability. He had to be able to do the job. He had to have both the spiritual gifts and the natural abilities to do what needed to be done.

In order to be faithful, a person has to have certain characteristics. He has to be committed. He has to be **committed to the renewal** of the Church in the power of the

Spirit. If a person did not believe in the message of the seminars (or even part of the message of the seminars), or if he were not dedicated to the spiritual renewal of the Church, or even if he did not see the importance of helping a person become firmly established in Christ, he would not be able to be faithful in his work in the seminars. He would not have the motivation to be faithful. He could not be relied upon. He might even be a hindrance to the people taking the seminars.

The team member also has to be **committed to his work in the seminar.** Before beginning, he should understand what is involved in being a team member and what kind of time he will have to set aside for it. The team leader should come to a clear agreement with the team member before he starts working on the team that he will do the work entrusted to him. If a person does not understand what he is being asked to do or if he does not agree to do it, it will be very difficult for him to be faithful as a team member.

The team member has to be **sound spiritually and emotionally.** People who are not living a good Christian life cannot do the work of a team member. People with serious psychological problems or emotional disturbances cannot do the work of a team member. Pastoral care of other people is not the right therapy for someone who cannot yet handle his own problems. A lack of spiritual and emotional soundness will show up in a lack of faithfulness to the work of being a team member.

The team member should be **mature in Christian living.** A person should be living what he is speaking about. Someone should be allowed to grow into Christian maturity before working on a Life in the Spirit Seminar team. And to some extent, maturity is a matter of time. It takes time for a person to develop maturity in Christian living.

A person, can, however, be faithful and not be able to

do a particular job. Many people who are sound and mature in Christian character and who are committed to the spiritual renewal of the Church and to their work in the seminars cannot do the work of the team member effectively.

In order to be able to do the work of a team member, a person has to **have the gifts for the job.** Some of these gifts are simply natural abilities which are not specifically Christian: the ability to speak with people without excessive fearfulness or shyness, the ability to speak clearly and explain well, the kind of personal strength that inspires respect. But the Lord also gives spiritual gifts or abilities that are really even more crucial than these: the ability to speak of the Lord in a way that can help people experience his reality, a spiritual discernment of where a person is in regard to the Lord and in regard to the work of evil spirits, a wisdom that provides a way of understanding what a person needs.

In the twelfth chapter of Romans, Paul writes about people who serve the Lord:

> "For by the grace given to me I bid every one among you not to think of himself more highly than he ought to think, but to think with sober judgment, each according to the measure of faith which God has assigned him. For as in one body we have many members, and all the members do not have the same function, so we, though many, are one body in Christ, and individually members one of another. Having gifts that differ according to the grace given to us, let us use them..."  (Rom 12:3-6)

A good Life in the Spirit Seminar team cannot be developed unless we accept the teaching of Paul that the Lord has not given everyone the gifts to do everything. That does not mean that one Christian is better than another. But it means that each Christian has a different place in the work of the whole Christian body. Many people are good candidates for working on Life in the Spirit Seminars, but many others, probably most people, are not.

It is true, the most common problem we will face today is not people thinking too highly of themselves, but rather people being too fearful. Often people are afraid to work on Life in the Spirit Seminars when the Lord has actually given them the gift. They have to understand that "God did not give us a spirit of timidity but a spirit of power and love and self-control" (II Tim 1:7). Nonetheless, there are still many people who should not work on Life in the Spirit teams, and some of them will be people who will want to. Those who choose the members of a team have to be convinced that we must choose those to whom the Lord has given the ability, and not "just anyone".

In addition to having the gifts, a team member must also have had the kind of experience which enables him to help others come into the full life of the Spirit. He should have **yielded to the gift of tongues himself.** It is very difficult for someone who has not yielded to the gift of tongues to help someone else to do so. Most often it is the sharing of our experiences with tongues that will help another person to yield, and very often that experience will give us the discernment that allows us to say the right thing to a person to help him yield to tongues.

The team member should also have **gone through the Life in the Spirit Seminars himself.** It is difficult to guide people through the seminars in the most fruitful way without having experienced it for oneself first. Even someone who has had experience in helping people be baptized in the Spirit by other means should go through the Life in the Spirit Seminars first before working on the team. The way the Lord works in the Life in the Spirit Seminars is different from most other approaches, and in order to cooperate with what the Lord is trying to do, a person should have experienced the seminars himself.

# THE TEAM MEMBER

**ROLE**
 — to be a leaven in the seminars, contributing life
    — praying actively
    — singing enthusiastically
    — following the instructions of the team leader promptly
    — being joyful
    — beginning conversation; befriending the people who come
    — listening attentively to the talks
 — to lead the discussion groups after the talks
 — to help, encourage, and counsel those taking the seminars
 — to pray with people to be baptized in the Spirit and to help them yield to the gift of tongues and prophecy
 — to pray for the seminars and the people in them

**TIME**
 — to come to each team meeting
 — to come to each seminar from the beginning to the end
 — to get together with each member of his discussion group between the fourth and the fifth week
 — sometimes, to contact those who miss seminars and to get together with them for make-up sessions

# THE TEAM LEADER

The team leader must have the same qualities of faithfulness and ability as the team member, but in choosing a team leader we are also choosing someone to be a pastor, a person who can take a group and form them into a community. He is responsible for the seminar as a whole and for the care of the people in it; he has the role of an elder in the Christian community. We are choosing someone to be a teacher, a person who can instruct new people clearly and powerfully in the basics of Christian life. The role of pastor and teacher demands special spiritual gifts (Eph 4:11). If the Lord is not working through the person in these ways, he will not be able to do the job which is needed.

In choosing a team leader, we must also choose someone who is mature and solid in the Christian life, someone who can command the respect of those in the seminar. His life should be marked by the same characteristics that Paul recommended for overseers (supervisors, bishops, elders) in the Christian community (Tim 3:1-7; Tit 1:7-9). These characteristics are listed in the table below.

Every team leader needs to be trained in working in the Life in the Spirit Seminars. The amount of training that he needs will depend upon his maturity as a Christian pastoral worker and leader. A mature worker who is already functioning as a pastoral leader in a charismatic group need only learn the way the Life in the Spirit Seminars work. On the other hand, someone who is just beginning to grow into pastoral and teaching leadership will need a good deal of experience in working in the seminars before he is able to lead one. He not only needs to learn about the operation of the program, but he must grow into maturity in his service of others.

Working in the Life in the Spirit Seminars is one of the best ways for someone who has a pastoral and teaching gift to begin to learn to grow into the use of the gift. The experience of helping others lay the foundation of a Christian life will impress upon the person the importance of a sound foundation in Christ. Many pastoral leaders in today's church find themselves trying to add second stories to Christian lives that have no foundation, a problem that a pastoral worker trained in the Life in the Spirit Seminars will more readily avoid. The Life in the Spirit Seminars also provide a place where a person can work directly with others and see the results of his efforts in a short period of time. He can more easily see if his efforts bear fruit, and he will learn that much more quickly.

# THE TEAM LEADER

**ROLE**
- to watch over the seminars and to see that everything is going well.
- to see that each person in the seminar is being cared for.
- to give many of the talks in the seminars, perhaps all; always to give the introductory talk, to lead seminar 5, and to give at least the last section of the closing talk.
- to form the team members into a team with unity of Spirit and an ability to work together for the Lord.
- to care for the team members and to help them learn to better serve the Lord.

**TIME**
- same as the team member, but with the added responsibility of preparation for the team meetings and talks.

**CHARACTER**
- above reproach (of impeccable character, of unquestionable integrity)
- not arrogant (not self-willed, not presumptuous)
- not quick tempered (not quarrelsome)

- not a drunkard (not a heavy drinker)
- not violent (not pugnacious, not hot tempered)
- not greedy for gain (not out to make money, not grasping)
- hospitable (a friend to those he does not know)
- a lover of goodness
- sensible (soberminded, discreet, master of himself)
- a man of prayer (holy)
- self-controlled (temperate)
- an apt teacher (capable, qualified to teach)
- he must manage his own household well . . .
- not a recent convert
- well thought of by outsiders
- holding firm to the sure word as taught

**TRAINING**
- go through the seminars as a regular team member
- work as an assistant to the team leader, giving some of the talks, helping in the preparation for the meetings
- give the seminars as a team leader with an experienced team leader working with him to help him in learning how to be an effective team leader
- actually take full responsibility as a team leader himself

# WORKING TOGETHER AS ONE

Spiritual power comes from unity in the Spirit. The more the Life in the Spirit Seminars team can come together in unity and in love for one another, the more powerful the effect they will have on the people who take part in the seminar. The unity and love of the team will protect the seminar against the work of the evil one, and will be a channel through which the power of the Holy Spirit can touch those participating in the seminar.

The unity of the team comes from having one mind

and one heart together. In his letter to the Philippians, Paul urged them to such oneness:

"Let your life be worthy of the gospel of Christ, so that whether I come and see you or am absent, I may hear of you that you stand firm in one spirit, with one mind striving side by side for the faith of the gospel."

(Phil. 1:27)

He went on even to plead with them to maintain that oneness:

"So if there is any encouragement in Christ, any incentive of love, any participation in the Spirit, any affection and sympathy, complete my joy by being of the same mind, having the same love, being in full accord and of one mind." (Phil. 2:1-2)

Behind this kind of oneness of mind and heart lies an attitude of love and humility. The team members love one another. As Peter put it in his first letter:

"Having purified your souls by your obedience to the truth for a sincere love of the brethren, love one another earnestly from the heart." ( 1 Peter 1:22-23)

The concrete expression of this love is a willingness to be servants. They have to humble themselves before one another, and serve one another, being willing to obey and willing to put the interests of others before their own. Paul continues in Philippians to:

"Do nothing from selfishness or conceit, but in humility count others better than yourselves. Let each of you look not only to his own interests, but also to the interests of others. Have this mind among yourselves which you have in Christ Jesus, who though he was in the form of God, did not count equality with God a thing to be grasped, but emptied himself, taking the form of a servant, being born in the likeness of men. And being found in human form he humbled himself and became obedient unto death, even death on a cross. Therefore God has highly exalted him and bestowed on him the name which is above every name..." (Phil 2:3-11)

The unity and love of the team members for one another is expressed both at the team meetings and at the seminars themselves. It is expressed in brotherly affection. The apostles frequently urged Christians to hug one another and to show their affection for one another (I Thess 5:26, I Peter 5:14, Rom 16:16, I Cor 16:20, II Cor 13:12). It is expressed in speaking words of exhortation and encouragement to one another (I Thess 5:11). It is expressed in teaching one another. It is even expressed in admonishing and reproving one another, helping one another to see what we have not done right (Col 3:16). Finally, it is expressed in praying for one another, not just at home, but also together.

Love should flow freely among us and be freely expressed if we are to have the spiritual unity and strength that the Lord is offering. In our contemporary society, we are often unable to freely express our love and support to one another. Letting the Lord teach us these things is part of growing in spiritual effectiveness as servants of the Lord.

# COMMUNICATION

In Paul's second letter to Timothy, we get a brief glimpse at the way that Paul and Timothy worked together. At the end of that letter, Paul speaks about some of the situations and problems that he and Timothy were then facing. He does not discuss these situations in broad and general terms, and he does not limit his advice to general instructions and exhortations. Instead, he talks about each concrete situation in a very exact and specific way. He tells Timothy where his co-workers are and what they are doing; he gives him specific instructions about what he is to do; he even tells him how to handle a specific individual he may encounter. Paul and Timothy worked by considering their actual situation in concrete and specific terms.

The most effective way for our Life in the Spirit Seminars team to work is to discuss things in the same way. We have to communicate with one another about each specific situation that confronts us: the incident that happened last week, the problem that a person in the seminar is having now, the things we need to do in the next session. We have to talk about each situation in a very concrete way—what is John's problem, how is it affecting him, what can we do to help? The team needs to come to a real oneness of mind about each specific situation. We should, of course, talk about these situations in a responsible way, with the appropriate confidentiality, especially when they involve areas of serious wrongdoing in lives.

This kind of communication and discussion will develop in us the pastoral discernment and judgment we need to be of real service to the people in the seminars. We are not really going to be able to help anyone if we learn all the general principles but cannot use them in actual situations. For example, we can be told that a person who is timid will have a hard time opening up to the work of the Spirit, but if we cannot recognize that someone is timid, that knowledge will not do anyone much good. We need to be able to judge situations and know how to deal with them, and the best way to develop this kind of pastoral judgment is to discuss what we think about each situation with the rest of the team. As we begin to discuss these situations in specific, concrete ways, there will usually be some disagreement among the team members. But we need not fear this disagreement; it is a sign that the Lord needs to show us something.

Team members can help one another grow in their ability to discern what is happening in different situations. If someone says, "Mary is not ready to be baptized in the Spirit", it is often good to ask that person what the grounds for that opinion are. It will sometimes happen that a person has been given a special sense about the situation by the Lord, a sense that cannot be easily expressed in words. But more often, people can give reasons for the judgments they make, especially if they ask themselves the question: "What things indicate to me that this is so?" If we carefully examine the grounds on which we form our opinions about the different situations and people in the seminars we will learn to recognize when we have formed our views on poor grounds and will be able to maintain a better perspective on what is really happening.

In order to be able to communicate effectively with one another, team members have to learn to observe what is happening in the seminars. In Acts 19, we have an example of how Paul worked in one situation:

> "While Apollos was at Corinth, Paul passed through the upper country and came to Ephesus. There he found some disciples, and he said to them, 'Did you receive the Holy Spirit when you believed?' And they said, 'No, we have never even heard that there is a Holy Spirit.' And he said, 'Into what then were you baptized?' They said, 'Into John's baptism.' " (Acts 19:1-3)

Paul then went on to tell them about Jesus, to baptize them and to pray for them to receive the Holy Spirit. Paul must have seen, as soon as he encountered these people, that though they seemed to be Christians there was something missing. So Paul asked them a simple question, a question that revealed what the situation really was. He asked them about their Christian past, about what had happened to them. Once they told him about their situation, he knew what to do.

Life in the Spirit Seminars team members have to be constantly observing what the true situation is. Besides staying in communication with one another, the team members have to stay in open communication with the people in the seminars. Like Paul we have to ask the people in the seminars what is happening to them in relation to the Lord and to the seminar. We have to know what has happened to them in order to know what they need from us.

Sometimes we can be blocked from finding out people's true situations by a fear of asking them specific questions. We may be afraid that they will be offended. In actuality, people are rarely offended by such questions if we ask them with genuine concern. We may be afraid that when the person answers a problem will appear that we cannot deal with. We need not fear our own inadequacies. The times when we are confronted with questions we cannot answer or problems we cannot handle are the times to open up and let the Lord teach us what to do.

We can also have a false view of faith that will act as a screen preventing us from seeing what is really happening. People sometimes feel that if we just have faith in the Lord, we can sit back and do nothing and the Lord will take care of everything in the seminar. It is true that the Lord wants us to put our faith in him and trust him to take care of everything in the seminar, but he does not want that faith to blind us from looking at the situation. Often the way he wants to work is to show us a need and to then teach us how to meet it.

Finally, the Life in the Spirit Seminars team has to communicate effectively about its own work for the Lord. The goal of our discussion of the seminars is to teach us how to work better in the seminars, to train us to be master builders for Christ. We should not be afraid of the truth. We have to discuss our work and its effect so that we keep on doing what we have done well, and change what we have not done well.

The team meeting is the place in which team members can communicate. If there is no team meeting or if it is only "administrative," that is, only concerned with the practical arrangements of the seminar, or even if it is only instructional, our work in the seminars will not be nearly as effective. The team must spend a good part of the team meeting discussing what is actually happening and in discussing particular situations.

## UNITED IN FAITH

When Paul described the aim he had when he began to work among the Corinthians, he said:

"When I came to you, brethren, I did not come proclaiming to you the testimony of God in lofty words or wisdom. For I decided to know nothing among you except Jesus Christ and him crucified. And I was with you in weakness and in much fear and trembling: and my speech and my message were not in plausible words of wisdom, but in demonstration of the Spirit and power, that your faith might not rest in the wisdom of men but in the power of God."

(I Cor 2:1-5)

His aim was to have the power of God working among the Corinthians. A spiritual change was needed. God had to do something to the Corinthians that no man could accomplish by himself. What the Corinthians needed is the same thing that people who come to the Life in the Spirit Seminars need—a change produced by a direct working of God.

The basis for letting God work through us in this way is the recognition of a fact: we cannot do what needs to be done ourselves. Only God can do it. As Paul said,

"Such is the confidence that we have through Christ toward God. Not that we are sufficient of ourselves to claim anything as coming from us; our sufficiency is from God, who has qualified us to be servants of a new covenant, made not in a written code, but in the Spirit; for the written code kills, but the Spirit gives life." (II Cor 3:4-6)

The Life in the Spirit Seminars are a work of the Spirit or

they are a failure. Only God can make it possible for us to bring new life in the Spirit to people. Only if we are servants of what he is doing and if he works through us can people experience a new spiritual life.

Yet this is precisely what God is offering us. He wants to work through us. We can expect him to be with us and to be at work both in us and in the people in the seminars. The basis of our service, therefore, has to be faith. As Paul said in his letter to the Galatians, "Does he who supplies the Spirit to you and works miracles among you do so by works of law or by hearing with faith?" The answer is clearly, "by hearing with faith" (Gal. 3:5). We have to know that the power of God is available to us and that we can expect to experience it working through us. We have to put our faith in him, and not just as individuals, but as a team. Jesus promised:

"Again I say to you, if two of you agree on earth about anything they ask, it will be done for them by my Father in heaven. For where two or three are gathered in my name, there am I in the midst of them." (Mt 18:19-20)

Our working in faith begins with prayer. The Life in the Spirit Seminars are built with prayer. We have to support the seminars with prayer, our prayer and the prayer of any others who will help us. And our prayer must be prayer in confidence. We know that God wants to work through us and that he wants to work in the people who come. We know that he is willing to work miracles among us. We know that he stands in our midst. "And this is the confidence which we have in him, that if we ask anything according to his will he hears us. And if we know that he hears us in whatever we ask, we know that we have obtained the requests made of him." (I John 5:14-15)

Faith is also essential to the team meetings and the seminar sessions themselves. We must learn to speak in faith and to act in faith. When we talk about problems in the seminar, we can speak about them in a way that expresses confidence that God will work, or we can speak fearfully and pessimistically. When we speak with the people in the seminar, we can speak to them in a way that conveys our assurance that God is present and will work with them, or in a way that conveys doubt and uncertainty. When the whole group comes together, in our prayer and in our speech, we can create an atmosphere of faith. Or we can allow the seminar to remain lifeless or perfunctory.

Finally, faith comes into our talking and praying with people in the seminars. The Lord is offering spiritual gifts to us. We can expect him to speak through us in prophecy, to give us discernment, to drive away evil spirits when we speak the word of command, to answer specific prayers when we pray over people, to guide us in what to say or do, to give us the word of wisdom or the word of knowledge we need, to reveal to us facts about the situation that we could not know otherwise. The Life in the Spirit Seminars can be charismatic, and they ought to be, or they will not have their full effect. There are few situations in which God is as eager to make the gifts of the Spirit available to us as the Life in the Spirit Seminars (or any situation in which he is seeking to reach people who do not know him). We can especially expect charismatic activity in the fifth week, when we pray with people. God's power can be present, if we but let him work through us.

# TEACHING
# AND DYNAMICS

Each Life in the Spirit Seminar is made up of a team meeting, a session which involves a talk and a discussion, supporting services, and sometimes make-up sessions. All of these elements play important roles in success of the seminars; they should not be viewed as independent of each other, but as an integrated whole.

## TEAM MEETING

The team meeting is almost the only opportunity that members of the seminar team have to discuss their work. It should be a time for support and encouragement, a time that builds the kind of unity, faith, and love discussed in the last chapter. If most of the meeting is devoted to administrative details, it will not have nearly the effectiveness it can have if the team spends the time in a concrete discussion of the problems and situations they are facing.

## TEAM MEETINGS

### PURPOSE

- to create a spiritual unity among the team members.
- to help the team members learn to better serve the Lord.
- to communicate about what is happening in the seminars.
- to prepare for each new seminar.

### FORMAT

- prayer for the seminars and the people in them
- a review of the last week's seminar
    - discussing any problems that appeared and what to do about them
    - going over the list of people to see how they are doing
- preview of next week's seminar
    - understanding the goal to be achieved
    - going over the format and the talk
- a discussion to learn how to serve well in the seminars

## TALKS

Most of the actual teaching that is done in the Life in the Spirit Seminars is done in the talks. These talks are short (20-25 minutes), yet three or four important points must be made in each one. If the speaker takes care in preparing and presenting his talk, following the guidelines in the table below, he can make these points clearly and powerfully, actually helping people to understand and accept them.

Each talk should be prepared with a special consideration for the people who will listen to it. The speaker should be sensitive to their needs and concerns, stating things in a way they will find clear. He should adopt an approach that they can accept, use examples they will understand, and speak in simple, everyday language. Personal testimony (how I came to see this point, how I figured out a way to do this myself, what this means to me) is particularly helpful, it not only demonstrates the practical meaning of our teaching, but it shows that the speaker considers these ideas important in his own life. (Four of these talks — the explanation session, the sign-up session, and seminars one and three — include an extended sharing of how the speaker turned to the Lord in a deeper way and found a deeper life in him. Some guidelines to follow in these sharings are also given below.)

Christianity seems to be surrounded with a number of controversies these days, but it is important for the speaker to avoid arguments and controversies in his talk. He should be sympathetic with others and not critical; criticism should be reserved only for sin and inadequate ideas. People and groups, especially churches, clergy, and religious practices, should never be criticized. On the other hand, the speaker should not be defensive or apologetic about the things he is saying; he should show his enthusiasm for the subject. His general approach should simply be: "This is true. It is something great that I have (recently) found out, and which you should want to know."

Above all else, the speaker should remember one thing: he can trust in the Lord. The Lord wants to hear his Word proclaimed, he wants to save men. He will give us the words we need:

"Now the word of the Lord came to me, saying, 'Before I formed you in the womb I knew you and before you were born I consecrated you; I appointed you a prophet to the nations. Then I said, 'Ah Lord God! Behold, I do not know how to speak for I am only a youth! But the Lord said to me: 'Do not say, '! am only a youth'; for to all to whom I send you you shall go and whatever I command you you shall speak. Be not afraid of them, for I am with you to deliver you, says the Lord.' Then the Lord put forth His hand and touched my mouth; and the Lord said to me, 'Behold, I have put my words in your mouth.' "

(Jer. 1:4-9)

# TALKS

**GUIDELINES FOR TALKS**

— Prepare your talk. Pray over it.

"Take heed to yourself and to your teaching; hold to that, for by so doing you will save both yourself and your hearers." (I Tim. 4:16)

— Use normal language, avoiding pious phrases, King James English, thee's and thou's, churchy jargon ("ministry," "edify," "saved"), etc.
— Say what you are saying; it is usually impossible to be too simple or blunt.
— Quote the scriptures, paraphrasing them if necessary to make the point.
— Use examples and stories from your own experience.

"When I came to you, brothers, I did not come proclaiming to you the testimony of God in lofty words or wisdom. For I decided to know nothing among you except Jesus Christ and him crucified. And I was with you in weakness and in much fear and trembling; and my speech and my message were not in plausible words of wisdom; but in demonstration of the Spirit and power, that your faith might not rest in the wisdom of men but in the power of God." (I Cor. 2:1-5)

— Avoid arguments, controversies, criticism of others.

"Have nothing to do with stupid, senseless controversies; you know that they breed quarrels. The Lord's servant must not be quarrelsome, but kindly to everyone, an apt teacher, forbearing, correcting his opponents with gentleness." (II Tim. 2:23-25)

— Don't moralize or preach, simply witness to the power of the Lord.

---

**GUIDELINES FOR PERSONAL TESTIMONY**
(In explanation and sign-up sessions, seminars one and three)

— Ask the Lord to give you wisdom and lead you in your sharing.
— Be brief, but present highlights of significant changes. Mention details of one or two of these changes to arouse interest.
— Talk over your experiences with someone else to see what part of them would be most helpful to others.
— Don't be wordy, beat around the bush, include irrelevant details, or emphasize how bad you used to be.
— Don't speak in glittering generalities. Avoid words like "wonderful," "glorious."
— Don't give the impression that the Christian life is "a bed of roses."

---

# DISCUSSIONS

Coming together in discussion groups in the right way is of tremendous importance for the success of the seminar. A warm, concerned group can set people free to respond to the Lord in new ways. The discussion leader should take special care to establish this atmosphere of love and interest in the group. He should be warm and friendly, get to know people and show his interest in them by remembering their names and the things they tell him. He should listen attentively to the things people say, and encourage those who are timid or shy to share and ask questions.

During the discussions, the role of the leader is to direct and encourage. He should help keep the discussion centered on the main points of the talk, but he should also encourage sharing and questions. If necessary, he should not be afraid to teach or explain some point, although he should not pretend to know all the answers. Many of the guidelines given above for speakers also apply to the discussion leader: sensitivity to the different people, concrete expression, sharing from experience, enthusiasm, not moralizing, avoiding controversies, speaking naturally, speaking in faith.

Of course, one key to successful discussion groups is setting up good groups at the beginning. There are two main principles to be followed here: put each person with the discussion leader who can help him the most, and be sure that each group can interact well as a whole.

There are some other principles to be kept in mind, although they are secondary to those above. Generally, people can identify best with a discussion leader of the same sex, and the leader can spot problems more easily in a person of the same sex. Also, many men find a woman discussion leader an impediment (this is not necessarily the time to confront this problem: first things first).

Spouses should usually be placed in separate discussion groups, although it is best if they attend the same seminar.

In separate discussion groups, they can often respond more freely to new ideas, but if they are in the same seminar they can also discuss things at home and move forward together.

People who have serious problems, or who are difficult to handle, should not be placed in groups with new team members. Ordinarily it is best not to put too many people with problems in one group, although it is sometimes worthwhile to form one group with all of them.

Finally, a person who shows special promise for working for the Lord, or who is in a particularly good position to reach others, should be placed with the discussion leader who can best win or encourage him.

# DISCUSSIONS

## SIZE

— Each group should have 3 or 4 people to each discussion leader. 5 is too many.

## PURPOSE

— To help people open up and respond to God's invitation
— To help them to understand and digest the material presented in the talk
— To give them a chance to ask questions
— To allow them to express their thoughts and feelings
— To provide an opportunity to deal with particular misconceptions and problems
— To support them in their efforts to find the truth
— To provide a place for them to begin to experience Christian community
— To see if the talks are being understood
— To find out where the group is at

## FORMAT

- The group forms and begins its discussion right after the talk.
- The discussion leader lets the group know that they are free to ask questions or bring up problems.
- If there are no questions or problems, the leader asks a question as a discussion starter, and asks each person in the group to share in answer to that question. (In the first few discussions, the leader should explain this approach to the group.)
- If the group is eager to respond to the talk, he allows them to, without bothering with the discussion starter.
- Sometime in the course of the discussion, he encourages them to ask questions or raise problems.
- When the leader asks the starter question, he should respond to it himself first; his response should be a model for what he would like their response to be.

# MAKE-UP SESSIONS

Each person should have all the materials that have been presented in the seminars when he is prayed with in the fifth week. Actually, he should be present for each session, since much of the growth in faith that must occur comes in the seminar sessions. If someone misses too many sessions, we should not hesitate to tell him to start another seminar, and anyone who misses a session should make it up.

If a number of people have missed a particular session, we might consider holding a special group make-up session. Individual make-ups should usually be given by the person's discussion leader. If this discussion leader is not also the team leader, he should bring a tape of the talk, play it, and then discuss it with the person; the team leader may also want to use the tape rather than give the talk, since it is difficult to give a full presentation to one person.

We should not feel that we have to make up sessions for everyone. Sometimes we simply lack the resources to do so. In most cases, it is not unreasonable to expect people to make the effort to be at all the sessions. If people with serious psychological or spiritual problems are absent, we should probably be less eager to make up sessions with them, unless we feel that the session or something else we can do will allow us to make a change in the problem. Their absence is probably a manifestation of their problem, and it will manifest itself in other ways further on. On the other hand, people who are in such a position that they could go on to help others might be worth extra effort (not because they deserve it any more, but because in helping them we will be helping many more people).

## MAKE-UP SESSIONS

**GUIDELINES**

— If a person misses the second session: we should suggest that he start over. (We can also recommend that he go to a seminar in its second week, but we should let the team leader of that seminar know ahead of time, and provide him with any background we have on the person.)

— If a person misses just the third or just the fourth session: we should try to make it up with him. Before we make up the third session with anyone, we should tell him that if he can not make the fourth session he should begin over when he can make them all.

— Exceptions to these guidelines can always be permitted for good reasons.

---

## AUXILIARY SERVICES

One person on the team should be designated as the helper. He is responsible for the setting of the seminars, the attendance roll and information transfer, and for selling literature at the seminar. The helper can also be a regular discussion leader.

These auxiliary services may seem minor, but they play an important part in the successful presentation of the seminars. If the setting is well arranged, people will find it easier to be involved in the seminar, and it will be that much easier for them to turn to the Lord. If the right kind of literature is available, it can further explain the teaching and build people's faith.

When selling literature, it is better to sell only a couple of books, preferably pamphlets and story-form books that are easily read. People are more likely to read the right books if only a few are recommended to them, and if they are made available in the seminars.

## AUXILIARY SERVICES

**SETTING**

— The chairs should be arranged to lead people to pay attention to the leader and to one another:
   — circular arrangements are best for a small group
   — semi-circular arrangements are best for larger groups
   — straight rows should be avoided unless the group is too large for anything else.

42

— The room should be well lighted and ventilated.
— There should be a blackboard for the speaker to use.

---

## INFORMATION TRANSFER

— The helper should take attendance, especially in a large group.
— He should collect a list of people with their names and addresses after the first session.
— If there are greeters, he should see that information is transferred to them. (Cf. pp. 181-182)

---

## RECOMMENDED LITERATURE

Christian books, pamphlets, and other material can be an important help to people in the Life in the Spirit Seminars. Team members can guide new people to helpful material at the book table at the weekly prayer meeting, or they can sell books at the seminar itself.

Every person in the seminars should own and use a Bible and the booklet *Finding New Life in the Spirit. Finding New Life in the Spirit* outlines a program of daily meditation and Scripture reading for the duration of the seminars. In addition, the seminar leader should recommend other Scripture readings at the conclusion of each talk.

Most people in the seminars need to grow in faith. Many need to be convinced that God loves them enough to give them the gift of his Spirit. David Wilkerson's *The Cross and the Switchblade* and John Sherrill's *They Speak With Other Tongues* are two books which describe the work of God's Spirit today with particular vividness.

Steve Clark's *Baptized in the Spirit and Spiritual Gifts* examines what scripture says about the gift of the Holy Spirit. Clark also discusses the theological terms we use to describe this experience. George Martin's *An Introduction to the Catholic Charismatic Renewal* is a brief, inexpensive description of the movement.

Toward the end of the seminars, team members should help people select reading matter which will help them grow in the Christian life. They should be told about *New Covenant,* a monthly magazine serving the worldwide charismatic renewal (P.O. Box 8617, Ann Arbor, Michigan 48107). A *New Covenant* subscription blank is found in the booklet *Finding New Life in the Spirit.*

Books which assist growth in the Spirit include *Growing in Faith* and *Knowing God's Will,* both by Steve Clark; *Live by the Spirit* by Michael Harper; *Hungry for God* by Ralph Martin; and *Reading Scripture as the Word of God* by George Martin. *Basic Christian Maturity,* a cassette album, provides a complete eight-session course on the fundamentals of the Christian life. These books and the cassette album are available from Charismatic Renewal Services, 237 North Michigan St., South Bend, Indiana 46601.

Some of the most useful books to assist basic growth in the Spirit are those in the *Living as a Christian* series, published by Servant Books. These books, all published in an inexpensive paperback format, are designed to provide the basic practical teaching Christians need to grow into spiritual maturity. The books in this series are grouped in sets covering basic maturity, overcoming obstacles, emotions, personal relationships, and growing in Christian character. For information write to Servant Publications, P.O. Box 8617, Ann Arbor, Michigan 48107. Many Christian bookstores stock individual titles in the series.

# THE NEW PEOPLE

Each Life in the Spirit Seminar is made up of more than a series of teachings and the team that presents them. It is made of people, individual people with unique personalities and problems, who have come to us to find out more about the new life that God is offering. They may have come for any number of reasons, from a real hunger for a new life to simple curiosity, but whatever their motivation, each one of them has been entrusted to us by the Lord. He loves them and his earnest desire is to see them receive his new life. If our desire is to serve the Lord, our overriding concern must be to give these people all the love and support they need.

In his first letter to the Thessalonians, Paul speaks about the way he worked to build up the Christians at

Thessalonica.

"We were gentle among you, like a nurse taking care of her children. So, being affectionately desirous of you, we were ready to share with you not only the gospel of God, but also our own selves, because you had become very dear to us...You know how, like a father with his children, we exhorted each one of you and encouraged you and charged you to lead a life worthy of God, who called you into his own kingdom and glory."

(I Thes 2:7-12)

Paul was a great teacher and preacher, he healed people and worked miracles, he received revelations from God and spoke them to the people. But he did not neglect the work of caring for each person individually, of talking to each one personally, of working to help each one serve God better and grow stronger in the Christian life.

In the Life in the Spirit Seminars we cannot neglect the work of caring for each person individually. The normal course of the seminars—the teachings, the contact with Christian life, being prayed with to be baptized in the Spirit—is enough in itself to take care of many problems. But each person will have other, unique needs that can only be met when he is individually cared for and spoken to and helped.

There are many ways we can give people individual attention in the seminars. Sometimes there are opportunities right in our discussion groups to speak to individual people and help them to work out problems or apply the message to their own lives. Sometimes informal contact with people, talking with them for a few minutes before or after the seminars, can make all the difference for them in opening up to the Lord. Sometimes we need to get together with someone at another time to help him work things out. We particularly need to meet with people like this after the fourth week, when we prepare them to be prayed with in the fifth week, but we can get together with someone anytime we see that they have a need for that sort of contact or feel the Lord leading us to meet with them.

## THE NEW PEOPLE

The work of individual attention begins when a person first comes to us, at the very beginning of the seminars. Our first duty to each person is to decide if our seminar is really going to help him to start a new life. Many people will come to us with problems that the Life in the Spirit Seminars are not designed to handle. Sometimes we will be able to help these people outside of the seminars, but at other times we won't. If we let the Lord teach us how to deal with the different types of people who come to us, we will be able to give each person as much help as we are equipped to give.

Each person is unique, and as we consider each individual we should remain prayerful and open to the leading of the Lord. But through our experience and through the counsel and teaching of the Lord, we can learn the best way to handle the different types of people who will come to us. Basically, there are four different types of people we have to consider.

THOSE WHO ARE READY TO ACCEPT THE LIFE OF THE SPIRIT THAT IS OFFERED IN THE SEMINARS AND WHO CAN Most of the people who will come to us are in this category. They will usually have different problems with accepting the new life the Lord is offering, sometimes simple human problems (fears, not wanting to change, resentment towards the Church, etc.), sometimes "theological"

(continued on next page)

problems (a bad image of "Pentecostals", putting limits on God's power, insufficient faith in his promises). Most normal problems are taken care of by the seminars.

**THOSE WHO ARE NOT YET READY TO MAKE A GENUINE COMMITMENT TO CHRIST OR TO SEEK A NEW LIFE IN THE SPIRIT** Some of these people have a problem with a genuine lack of faith or unwillingness to repent, others are troubled by serious theological reservations. Our ability to help them varies in each case. If we have the resources in our community to deal with their problems (someone who can talk with them, another course that will bring them to faith, etc.) we should probably help them resolve their difficulties before they begin the Life in the Spirit Seminars. Sometimes we can recommend the right book to help them, and suggest that they read that and then come to the seminars when they feel ready. But if we don't have any other help to offer them, we have to seriously consider and decide if this person will be brought closer to Christ by the Life in the Spirit Seminars, or whether he will react negatively and become more hardened.

**THOSE WHO COME FROM OUT OF TOWN** Often we should not take people from out of town into our seminars. If the Life in the Spirit Seminars are given in a place closer to their home, we should send them there. In order to grow in the new life, they need to join together with people who live near them. If we take them into our seminar they will form their ties with our group and it will be harder for them to become part of another group. This can make it much harder for them to continue to grow.

(continued on next page)

**THOSE WITH SERIOUS PSYCHOLOGICAL PRO—
BLEMS** There are different types of serious psychological problems and different things that we can do
for these people. In general, a community has to be
fairly mature before it can be of any real help to
people with serious psychological problems. The Lord
can equip us to help with every problem, but if we
take on someone's problems before he gives us the
gifts to handle them we are likely to end up in a
situation that drains us and does not help the other
person (like long counseling sessions, inviting them to
live with us, etc.). If a person is disruptive, imbalanced
(i.e., has a history of "breaks"), or if his behavior is
an obstacle to other people in opening up to the Lord,
we should ask him not to come to the seminars. On the
other hand, if someone has a serious psychological
problem but can function normally, the Life in the
Spirit Seminars will probably be helpful to him.
Wisdom and discernment are needed in these situations.

God can do everything; Jesus can help every man. But
sometimes he says to us: "That is not a service that I have
given you the gifts to perform." Paul said in Romans, "I bid
every one of you not to think of himself more highly than
he ought to think, but to think with sober judgement, each
according to the measure of faith which God has assigned
to him" (Rom 12:3). We cannot help every one in the Life
in the Spirit Seminars, and we will often have to tell people
that this is not the right place for them. Sometimes that will
be because the seminars themselves are not designed to help
every person, sometimes because our community or prayer
group is not able to help them. God wants to see Christian
communities, bodies of Christ, grow up that can help every
person who comes to them. But we have to know when we

have grown to that point and when we are not yet there, we have to recognize which gifts we have and which we have not received.

The first step, then, of our work of individual contact is to discern which people cannot be helped by our Life in the Spirit Seminars and to try to help them find the right place. The initial group that comes to us is probably not the group that should make up the seminar. It is when we have the right group, those who are ready for what the Lord wants to do in the seminars, that the seminars can be most powerful.

## THE PROCESS

Each person who should be in the seminars will bring two things with him when he first comes. First of all, he will already have some real faith, even if he doesn't realize it himself. Jesus said, "No one can come to me unless the Father who sent me draws him." (Jn 6:44). We can count on the fact that these people are in our seminars because God has already begun to work in them and is drawing them to himself.

But at the same time, each person brings with him some problems and obstacles that can keep him from fully turning to the Lord—things like personal difficulties, theological questions, a lack of knowledge about Christianity. Our main service as Life in the Spirit team members is not to solve all of the problems people have when they come to the seminars, although when we can solve them or give them significant help we should. But our main responsibility is to help and encourage them to have faith in the Lord and to decide to obey the Lord in a new way. Our task is to help them to take the first step of a new relationship with Jesus.

When we consider each person and his problems, we have to keep our true responsibility to him in mind. People can have many problems, from theological problems to personal problems, which will not keep them from opening up to a new relationship to the Lord. Our responsibility is to see that they are able to overcome those problems which really are obstacles to their acceptance of the new life

Just being in the Life in the Spirit Seminars will begin a process of growth in each person which will overcome their obstacles. As people begin to hear and understand God's word through the teaching in the seminars, their wrong attitudes will dissolve and they will be able to approach the Lord in a better and better way. The experience of Christian life in the seminars and in our communities and prayer groups will also make a big difference. Our personal contact with people will be a major help in overcoming their obstacles; just sharing with them our faith and encouragement and our knowledge of the right way to take the first step with the Lord is going to help them take that first step themselves.

This process of growth in the Life in the Spirit Seminars can be divided in two parts—the first five weeks of the seminars and the last two. In the first five weeks, up to the night when people are prayed with to be baptized in the Spirit, that process should be aimed at two things. The first is fostering faith in the people—faith has to "catch" in them. They have to come to an inner assurance that the Lord will come to them and baptize them in his Spirit; they have to reach the inner belief that God will be true to his promises.

The second thing is that each person has to authentically commit himself to Jesus Christ as Lord. He has to come to the heart decision that he will obey Jesus and live the Christian life, he has to renounce all serious wrongdoing and give his life to Jesus. Repentance is an essential step to being baptized in the Spirit.

It can often happen that a person will have genuine faith and repentance without really knowing it. Feelings of doubt can exist at the same time as true faith, wayward desires and feelings of rebellion can still trouble someone who has genuinely repented. These doubts and feelings and desires will sometimes blind a person to the real changes happening in his heart. Sometimes we will be able to recognize someone's faith and repentance before he can, but sometimes neither he nor we will be able to see it. Nonetheless, before someone can be baptized in the Spirit and begin to lead a new life, he must have genuine faith and repentance.

Once a person has reached faith and repentance, it is an easy matter to help them to receive the release of the Spirit in their lives. Our concern then, has to be to help them to turn to the Lord in faith and repentance, to turn toward the Lord with the right kind of openness.

People do not catch faith or come to a decision to follow the Lord in any particular week. Some people come to the seminar prepared; we could pray with them the first night and they would easily yield to the Spirit. Some do not reach that point until the moment when hands are actually laid on them and the Lord does something to them; that is often the moment when they turn to the Lord in faith and decision. We do not need to know when the change is made. Sometimes we will be able to see it in the way they respond to the talks and the things we say, sometimes we will not. But our ability to discern the point they are at is not as important as our realization that the process of growing in faith and obedience is going on inside them. It is that process that we have to serve.

After the fifth week, our concern changes somewhat. We still need to be concerned with faith and obedience. What happened in the fifth week needs to be fostered. Part of our major concern in the last two weeks must be to encourage people to continue with the step they took, to become firmer in faith and obedience. If we ever forget that every Christian has to grow in faith and obedience all the time, and needs encouragement to do so, we will be very poor workmen in building Christian communities and helping Christians to grow.

But there is another concern after the fifth week that we have to direct much of our attention to. The last two weeks are the crucial time for people in the seminars to make concrete decisions to connect themselves to a community or prayer group in a way that will allow them to receive the help they need to grow in the life of the Spirit. Our service as team members has to aim at encouraging them to make the definite decision to become part of a community or prayer group in a way which will help them to grow. We are the servants of what God is doing. As Paul said in I Corinthians:

"What then is Apollos? what is Paul? Servants through whom you believed, as the Lord assigned to each. I planted, Apollos watered, but God gave the growth. So neither he who plants nor he who waters is anything, but only God who gives the growth. He who plants and he who waters are equal, and each shall receive his wages according to his labor. For we are fellow workers for God; you are God's field, God's building."

(I Cor 3:5-9)

God is at work in the Life in the Spirit Seminars, in a new way drawing men to himself and building them into the life of his people. We do not have to feel that we have to "get people baptized in the Spirit" or "get them to the Lord". God himself will do it, and he will work through a number of means that are in the seminars. We just have to make ourselves available to him as his servants so that we can do the part of the work that he has assigned to us. He may want us to plant a seed, he may want us to water a plant, or to hoe, or to prune or to do any of a number of things. Our task is to do that which will serve the process of a person's turning to him.

---

These are some of the problems which can block people from turning fully to the Lord:

**LACK OF KNOWLEDGE** Often people will have hazy ideas about the Christian life or about being baptized in the Spirit. By the fifth week, their ideas should be clear enough so that they can make a genuine commitment to Christ and ask for what God is promising.

**PERSONAL DIFFICULTIES** Sometimes people can be bothered by personal difficulties which get in the way of their yielding to the Lord. The kinds of difficulties which get in the way are numerous—psychological problems, problems in their family or living situation, financial problems, and so on. If we are aware of the difficulties, we can help people get through them—and we can help them open up to the work of the Lord in the midst of the problem.

**"THEOLOGICAL SCREENS"** People will often say things like "Sure the Holy Spirit will work in some people's lives—but he does not want me to experience his presence the way he wants other people to". Or maybe, "The gifts of the Spirit are just for some people". Or perhaps, "The Lord just wants us to pray that his will be done. He doesn't want us to pray for things for ourselves". Or "Having a spiritual gift would make me proud". In such cases people are putting limits on what the Lord can do for them, and we need to help them see the fullness of his power and love. We

(continued on next page)

---

have to help them to see that he wants them to experience him, and he wants to work through them powerfully.

**RELIGIOUS EXPERIENCE SEEKING** From time to time we encounter people who look upon baptism in the Holy Spirit as a "religious experience" which is good to have. To these people we have to point out that being baptized in the Spirit prepares us for a deeper Christian life and involved in it is a serious commitment to live a Christian life and to service.

**LACK OF WILLINGNESS** People are sometimes willing to go part way with the Lord—but not all the way. This is most noticeable in connection with the gift of tongues. If people do not have a real eagerness for *all* that the Lord will do, then they will not end up living the Christian life as they ought.

# THE COMMUNITY

A carpenter could make a beautiful door, the most beautiful door in the world, and that door could turn out useless to a house. It might be too big, or too wide, or too thin. There might be any number of things wrong with it. There's no guarantee that an excellent door is going to be able to be part of a house. For that, the eye of an architect (or a "master builder") is needed. The door does not only have to be beautiful and well-made. It has to fit into the house and make the house a better house. The carpenter has to build the door according to the specifications of the house.

The same thing is true of the Life in the Spirit Seminars. What the Lord wants is not excellent Life in the Spirit Seminars. What he wants is for his people to be built up and made strong. Just as a beautiful door would be useless to a house if it could not be fit into the house, so the Life in the Spirit Seminars may turn out to be of little value if they do not fit into what God is building in a particular place.

The Life in the Spirit Seminars are designed to be an introduction to a new life in the Spirit that is lived with others. Experience shows that if a person does not make connection with a group of other people living this new life, the Life in the Spirit Seminars will not make a major difference in his life. The new life he has begun will fade away. The Life in the Spirit Seminars all by themselves are not effective in the long run. More is needed.

It therefore only makes sense to think of the Life in the Spirit Seminars as one instrument in the life of some community or prayer group. The seminars are designed as an evangelistic teaching method which helps people enter the life of a community or prayer group. As such they have to be related in the right sort of way to the life of the community or prayer group they are part of.

There are many types of groups who make use of the Life in the Spirit Seminars. Some of them are just small prayer groups who only put on seminars from time to time when a few people collect who want them. Usually such seminars have only three or four people in them and it is an easy matter for these few people to become a regular part of the prayer group. Some of the groups who use the seminars are large communities or renewal centers who serve many people over a wide geographical area. Such groups begin new seminars each week and have ten or twenty people in each seminar from widely scattered localities. For these groups, integrating the seminars into the communities in such a way that the people in the seminars find it easy to go on can be a complex task. There are, of course, a variety of different types of groups in between, and each type of group has to relate the seminars to their group in a slightly different way.

There are, however, a number of things that every group has to attend to, no matter how large or how small the group. The first is *attracting the right people* to the seminars. What we want in the seminars are people who are ready to turn to the Lord in a deeper way and be baptized in the Spirit. They may not have to be ready to be baptized in the Spirit the first week, but they have to be open. They have to be seriously interested. Ordinarily we do not want the skeptical, the merely curious, or the person who is not open to entering into or deepening a committed relationship with Christ.

Part of the way of getting the right people is announcing the seminars in the right way. When we announce them at meetings, we give people an idea of what to expect. The way we announce the seminars helps them decide whether they want to begin. If we want people who are interested in a change in their personal relationship with the Lord, we should say that. If we want people who are considering baptism in the Spirit, we should say that. If we do not want people from out of town, we should say that too. We should also give relevant concrete details: how many weeks it will be, when the sessions will be held, how long the sessions are.

Another part of the way of getting the right people is educating the prayer group or community in who should come. Most people come on other people's encouragement. If we find that the people who are coming to begin the seminars are coming before they are ready, we should explain that to the others in the group. The more the community as a whole understands who should come, the more likely it is that the right people will be there.

Sometimes when a problem exists with the people who come, it stems from the way people have been told. When people are pressured to come, often they are not open to the Lord. Or when people are encouraged to begin without being told what they are getting into, they often begin unprepared to take part. The prayer group or community often needs to be educated in how to invite people and encourage them.

Every group also needs to pay attention to *knitting the people who come to the seminar into the life of the community.* The transition has to be made from the seminar to becoming part of the prayer group or community. Many will not continue past the Life in the Spirit Seminars without help. In order to go on, they have to be encouraged in the seminars to go on. The last two weeks of the seminar should make this a special concern. They also have to be drawn into the life of the community. Many times, the difference between someone staying and going is simply some personal contact with others in the prayer group or community. When bonds are formed and love grows, a person is much more likely to be willing to go on. People especially need to get to know others outside of formal meeting times. In smaller groups, the team members can take this responsibility. In larger groups, a system of "greeters" is needed. (see pp. 173-183)

Thirdly, every group has to attend to the "structural tie-in" to the community. Because the Life in the Spirit Seminars are so important a part of the life of the prayer group or the community, they must be well integrated. Some small group of people should not decide on their own to offer Life in the Spirit Seminars. Those who have the overall responsibility for the group should take responsibility for the seminars. They should appoint the team leaders and the teams. They should see that the seminars are preparing people properly for the life of the prayer group or community. They should make it their concern that someone is responsible for information flow between the seminars and others in the community (the leaders in the prayer group or community should know who is in the seminar and who was prayed with; others in the groups should know of new people in the seminars who live near them or are in their parish or church; the greeters should know by the second week who is in the seminar and there should be regular communication between them and the discussion leaders).

Finally, every group has to attend to *what is needed after the seminars.* The seminars are not enough. People need much more help than the seminar gives. Different groups can do different things. Large, mature communities can provide further courses and helps of various kinds. Smaller groups or newer groups often can do little more than take people into their life and share with them books and tapes and personal love and encouragement. We can only do what the Lord assigns to us, but nonetheless we need to make growth beyond the seminars our prayerful concern.

# GREETERS

In larger communities, the work of caring for people can be divided between Life in the Spirit Seminars team members and "greeters". "Greeters" are a group of people who take on the responsibility of helping people who come to the Life in the Spirit Seminars to be integrated into the life of the community. They contact the new person after the second week and begin to invite them to places at which they can make contact with the life of the community or prayer groups (smaller prayer groups, parties, liturgies or special services, places at which community members gather). They will often make an effort to introduce them to people in the community and to have them invited to dinner. A main concern is to see that the new people experience what Christian life means on a daily basis (and not just at meetings) and to see that they do not feel left out.

Each week the greeter will try to talk to each person he is responsible for, not necessarily for a long period of time. The greeter takes the responsibility to see that the person does not get lost and does not lack the help he needs up to the point where he is a part of the community or prayer group. It is especially important that the greeter keep in contact with the person for a period of time after the seminars are over so that the person can make the transition from the seminars without getting lost.

# PART TWO

# **THE SEMINARS**

# The Explanation Session

---

## GOAL

To give a brief, clear explanation of the Christian message so that people can see the things that lie behind their experience at the meeting and be attracted towards turning to the Lord and entering the Life in the Spirit Seminars.

---

The explanation session is not necessarily part of the Life in the Spirit Seminars. Many communities and prayer groups, however, have found it valuable to have explanation sessions before their open meeting, after their open meeting, or both. The explanation session provides an opportunity to give people a brief explanation of "what's going on around here" and allows them to ask any questions they may have. It is a way of drawing people to the Lord.

The explanation session can either be handled by a team of people who are responsible only for the explanation session, or it can be handled by the same team that is responsible for the Life in the Spirit Seminars. A Life in the Spirit Seminars team could give the explanation session for the week or two before they begin their seminar.

# The Team Meeting

1.  Discuss the explanation session
    —go over the talk and the format
    —go over the team member's role
    —share about the type of people who might come and the approach the team should take
2.  Pray for the session and the people who will come

# The Explanation Session

A.  **Preliminaries**
    1. Greet the people while waiting to begin
    2. Get the names and addresses

B.  **The Presentation**
    **Introduction:**
    —the speaker introduces himself
    —he speaks about the community/prayer group and the explanation session
    1. God loves you and wants you to live a full, happy life.
    2. Man is sinful and separated from God and therefore he cannot know God's love and share in God's life with others.
    3. Jesus Christ is the only one who can give you power to live this new life. Through him you can know God's love and share in God's life with others.

4. You must accept Jesus Christ into your own life as Lord and Savior and then you can be baptized in the Holy Spirit and so experience the power to live a new life.

Recommend the Life in the Spirit Seminars.

C. Question And Answer Period

1. If the group is large enough, the leader splits it into groups led by a team member.
2. The leader encourages questions.
3. If it has not been mentioned, the leader speaks about the gift of tongues at more length.
4. The leader closes by recommending further reading.

# COMMENTS ON THE DYNAMICS

The explanation session is designed to be short (20-25 minutes of talk with 30 minutes of questions and answers). The speaker does not need to add much to the expanded outline of the talk.

The question and answer period is best handled by splitting into small groups of seven or eight with a team member in each group to handle questions. If the speaker is alone or with too few others to form groups, the questions can be handled in one large group. The team member should expect to get some rough questions (will people who never heard of Jesus be condemned to hell? how come the pope said...?, etc.). They should not try to answer questions that they cannot answer. Insofar as possible they should try to keep the discussion centered on the basic Christian message.

Only a small number of books should be recommended at the end. The books recommended for the first session of the Life in the Spirit Seminars would also be appropriate for the explanation session. (Cf. p. 43)

# THE EXPLANATION SESSION

# Expanded Outline
## of the Presentation

**Introduction:**

Tonight you are going to participate (have participated) in a Christian community meeting/prayer meeting. We are a community of Christians who have been trying to live a Christian life much like that of the Christians in the early Church.

We are people who have begun to experience the reality of Jesus and the power of the Holy Spirit transforming and changing our whole life.

I am going to say some things about our understanding of what it means to be a Christian and what it means to be baptized in the Spirit, and then we'll take time for questions and answers.

**The message of Christ**

In order to understand what we are experiencing it is necessary to understand the basic message of Jesus. To summarize this message briefly I want to present what we call "The Four Basic Truths". This is a four-point summary of the basic elements of the gospel.

**Truth 1: God loves you and wants you to live a full, happy life.**

(Christ speaking) "I came that they might have life and have it abundantly" (Jn 10:10).

God wants us to know him and experience his love and live together in a community of love with all men.

Why is it that most people do not experience this kind of life?

67

**Truth 2:** Man is sinful and separated from God and therefore he cannot know God's love and share in God's life with others.

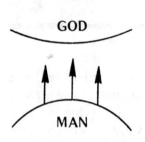

Men are continually trying to reach God by their own efforts: ethics, philosophy, drugs, religion, etc.

"All have sinned and come short of the glory of God" (Rom 3:23).

(Sin involves indifference to God and is characterized by actively or passively rebelling against God.)

Man's separation from God results in man's separation from man.

"Because men refuse to acknowledge God. . . they are full of all kinds of wickedness, greed, and hate" (Rom 1:28).

Men cannot live together in love and peace unless there is first a spiritual change in them which only God can produce.

How does this spiritual change take place?

**Truth 3:** Jesus Christ is the only one who can give you power to live this life. Through him you can know God's love and share in God's life with others.

"God so loved the world that he sent his only son, that whoever believes in him should not perish but have eternal life" (Jn 3:16).

In Jesus, God became man and entered the world to overcome the separation between God and man. Through his life, death and resurrection Jesus Christ has made it possible for men to experience this abundant life.

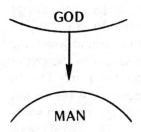

"I am the way, the truth and the life: no man comes to the Father but through me" (Jn 14:6 ).

Through Jesus Christ, God gives men the power to live together with the kind of love and harmony which God intended for mankind.

More is needed than just knowing this...

**Truth 4:** You must accept Jesus Christ into your own life as Lord and Savior and then you can be baptized in the Holy Spirit and so experience the power to live a new life.

**Accepting Christ:**

Accepting Christ into your life is more than just believing that he was God and died for men and more than just doing good works and following his (moral) teaching. It means entering into a personal relationship with Christ in which we receive his love and give our life to him.

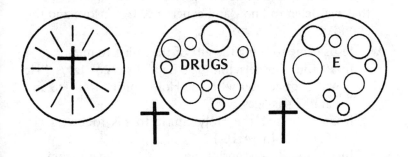

Each circle represents a man's life. The center of the circles represents the center of the life — the driver's seat, the point from which the life is controlled, around which the life centers. Whoever or whatever is seated in the center is the person or thing that controls the man's life. In most people's lives it is the self or ego that is the center. Sometimes it is another person, or drugs, or even some cause. There are many interests in each man's life — school, family, work, art, music, etc. (the other circles.) Christ may be one of the interests in this man's life (the cross inside the circle), or he may be entirely outside of the life as is the case with someone who's never heard of him or seriously considered him. A person like this does not experience God's presence and love. He experiences a lack of goal and power, a lack of real peace and joy. If he considers himself a Christian he finds his Christianity empty and meaningless.

To accept Jesus Christ into your life means to allow him to take the center. It involves surrendering your life to him. When we do this, we can come to know him personally.

"But to all who received him, who believed in his name, he gave power to become children of God " (Jn 1:12).

### The gift of the Spirit

The gift of the Spirit fills our whole life and changes us so that we begin to know and experience God's love and the abundant life Jesus spoke of.

A.  Jesus came to bring the gift of the Spirit to men
In all four Gospels John the Baptist says of Jesus, "He will baptize you with the Holy Spirit" (Mk 1:8 and parallel passages).

Jesus promised the Holy Spirit to his followers (Jn 16:12-13, Jn 14:16-17).

Just before his ascension he said, "You heard from me that John baptized with water, but before many

days you shall be baptized with the Holy Spirit"
(Acts 1:5).

B. The power of the Spirit was evident in the early
Church
1. Pentecost
   — the promise fulfilled (Acts 2:4)
   — the difference: boldness, power, unity, love,
   effective preaching of the gospel, conversions
   — manifestations of the Spirit: tongues, inspired praise of God
2. After Pentecost
   One could mention any of the following: Philip
   in Samaria (Acts 8), Paul and Ananias
   (Acts 9), Peter and Cornelius (Acts 10),
   Paul at Ephesus (Acts 19); or from St. Paul:
   Gal 3:1-5, or 1 Thess 1:2-10.
   Conclusion: experiencing the power of the
   Spirit in a variety of manifest ways was
   normal in the lives of the early Christians.
   People were really changed by the gift of the
   Holy Spirit, and the changes were such that
   both they themselves and other people could
   tell that they were different.

C. The church has never lost the life of the Spirit nor the
experience of the power of the Spirit. But its history
has seen periods both in which the life of the Spirit
seemed to slacken, and in which there was growing
spiritual renewal. Today, in the Catholic Church
there is growing spiritual renewal, which seems to be
an answer to the prayer which Pope John asked
Catholics to say before and during the Second Vatican Council: "Renew in our day, O Lord, your wonders as in a new Pentecost." In the years following
the Council, a great many Catholics have come to a
release or a renewal in their experience of the power

of the Spirit. This spiritual renewal among Catholics is paralleled in practically all Christian churches. Millions of Christians are experiencing the same power of the Holy Spirit that marked the early church. (Here describe the kind of difference the Holy Spirit makes in the life of a Christian with examples under such headings as these:)

1. prayer life changes — the reality of God in prayer
2. scripture — how the Spirit makes it alive
3. telling others about Christ — coming from new knowledge of Jesus
4. Christian community — new life shared
5. the gifts of the Spirit
   a. tongues — a gift of prayer which most receive when they are baptized in the Spirit
   b. prophecy—speaking in the first person a message inspired by the Holy Spirit—a way for God to speak to us, usually intended for the "upbuilding, encouragement, and consolation" of a prayer group or community (cf. 1 Cor 14:3), or for some kind of guidance (cf. Acts 11:27-30; 13:2-4).
   c. other gifts, such as those described in 1 Cor 12:4-11 and Rom 12:6-8.
6. the fruits of the Spirit (Gal 5:22): the Holy Spirit begins to produce changes in character and attitudes such that we begin to be able to act as Christ did.

The life in the Spirit is available for everyone. Those who are Christians have already received the gift of the Spirit, but oftentimes their experience of the Holy Spirit does not correspond to that described in the New Testament.

The Life in the Spirit Seminars provide a way to learn more about life in the Spirit and be baptized in the Spirit. (Describe the Seminars briefly and indicate when the next one starts.)

# COMMENTS ON THE PRESENTATION

The speaker does not need to add much to this expanded outline. The most important addition he should make is his own personal testimony, which should be given in section C. of the talk, while describing the kind of difference the Holy Spirit makes in the life of a Christian. In fact, the whole last section could be given as a personal testimony.

In giving personal testimony, the speaker should describe the kind of life he led before accepting the lordship of Christ in his life or before being baptized in the Spirit. He should share how he came to accept Jesus as his Lord, and how he was baptized in the Spirit. He should then share the kind of changes that he has seen in his life since then. Do not speak in generalities. When possible, the speaker should tell the story of his turning to the Lord and should add incidents which illustrate the points which he is trying to make. The testimony should be short and simple.

Much of the power of the talk given in the explanation comes from its directness and simplicity. The speaker does not have to elaborate a great deal: the message can speak for itself in a powerful way. The diagrams help a great deal in making the points clear and powerful. The speaker can make many of the points by drawing the diagrams (or parts of the diagrams) and explaining them. The scriptural stories and testimony will make the last sections of the talk effective.

# The Sign-Up Session

---

## GOAL

To provide a way for people to sign up for the seminars, to motivate people to take the seminars, to prepare them to begin the seminars with the right attitudes.

---

Like the explanation session, the sign-up session is not necessarily part of the Life in the Spirit Seminars. It is, however, a good method for signing people up for the seminars in a way which will motivate them to begin them and which will prepare them psychologically and spiritually for what the seminars are.

There are three methods we can use to assemble a group of people to take the seminars. The first is to simply announce the time and place for the first session and accept everyone who comes into the seminar. The second is to have a list or registration cards on which people can sign up beforehand. The third is to have a sign-up session.

The two methods that allow people to register before-hand, the sign-up list and sign-up session, have a number of advantages: they provide advance information on the size and composition of the group; they make it possible to schedule seminars as they are needed; they help us to assign the right type of team members in the proper number; and they make it possible for us to sort out those people whom we cannot serve (those people from out of our area, etc.). When we have some sort of pre-registration, we can bring together for the first session a group that is more likely to last through all the seminars. The sign-up session improves the quality of the participation of the people who come to the seminars, and makes it more likely that they will stay until the end.

# The Team Meetings

Generally, one special team is assigned to work on the sign-up sessions for some period of time. It is not necessary that they meet together every week of this time, but there should be a team meeting at the beginning of their period of service, another at the end, and one or two evaluation sessions during the time they are working together.

# The Initial Team Meeting

1.  Go over the format of the sign-up session
2.  Explain the role of the team members
    — to greet people and help them feel relaxed before and after the session (team members should be in the room before the people arrive)
    — to share with people informally
    — to give personal sharings
3.  Discuss how to give a personal sharing (see p. 29)
4.  Plan a schedule of sharings; appoint an "usher" to direct people to their seats and maintain order.

# Evaluation Sessions

During their term of service, it is valuable for the team to meet once or twice to evaluate the session and discuss how it can be improved. Some questions that can help us in our evaluation are:

- how did the leader do in describing the seminars to people?
- how were the personal sharings?
- how did the practical arrangements work out?

# The Final Meeting

1. Evaluate the sign-up session for the whole period.
2. Share what the Lord did with us or taught us while we were working on the sign-up session.
3. Pray for all the people who came.

The team leader should communicate the results of the evaluation to the people in the community who are responsible for the area.

# The Sign-Up Session

A. The leader's introduction
   1. Explain the sign-up briefly.
   2. By asking for a show of hands, find out how many people have to leave immediately. Tell them they may do so as soon as they sign up.
   3. Give a short description of the seminars.

B. **The sign-up**

  1. Distribute the sign-up cards.
     - encourage them to answer all the questions
     - ask those from "out of the area" to speak to the leader afterwards
  2. Collect the cards.
  3. Permit those who had indicated that they need to leave early to go.

C. **The sharing**

  1. A perspective on the seminars
  2. God is at work in the seminars
  3. Individual sharings by members of the team

D. **Conclusion**

  1. Begin now to open your life in a new way to Jesus and to the work of the Holy Spirit.
  2. The leader invites the people to pray silently with him; he asks Jesus aloud to begin to work in their lives.
  3. Recommend literature for them.
  4. If possible, tell them when they can begin the seminars.

# COMMENTS ON THE DYNAMICS

The sign-up session should be relatively brief, not much more than half an hour altogether. The tone should be welcoming — warm, open, and friendly. The normal time to hold the session would be after the main gathering of the community or prayer group. Should the gathering go later than usual, the session can be briefer.

The team members should be at the sign-up session room immediately after the end of the gathering. They should introduce themselves to the people who have come to sign up and talk with them informally. They should also be available to talk with people at the end of the session. It is a good idea to have refreshments available and to hold the session in a room that is inviting and comfortable.

The individual sharings should be given by two or three team members. If possible, it is good to have a variety of sharings: a younger person and an older person, a person who was not a practicing Catholic before he took the seminars, and a person who was already a practicing Catholic, but was baptized in the Spirit during the seminars.

The leader should plan a rotating schedule for the individual sharings if the team is larger than three people. He should be open to adjusting that schedule according to the type of people who come to the sign-up session. (If there are a large number of college students, for instance, a sharing from a college student would help.)

Only a small number of books should be recommended at the end of the session. The books recommended for the introductory session would also be appropriate for the sign-up session.

# THE SIGN-UP SESSION

# Expanded Outline
## of the Presentation

**A.   Short description of the seminars**

They last for seven weeks.

They meet for about one hour every _____ evening at _____ p.m.

During the first four weeks we hear about the promises of Christ and the way we can respond to them, how we can be baptized in the Spirit, how we can yield to spiritual gifts, etc.

The fifth week is a prayer session for those who are ready to be prayed with to be baptized in the Spirit.

The last two weeks teach us about growing in the life of the Spirit.

The seminars are for everyone—whether he has been a committed Christian up to now or not, whether he has already been baptized in the Spirit or not.

**B.   The sharing**

1.  A perspective on the seminars:

They were developed several years ago to help people come into a deeper life in the Spirit. They were developed in this format as the Lord showed us that he desires not only that we turn our lives to Christ and be baptized in the Spirit, but also that we should live a new "life in the Spirit" together with other Christians. They provide a chance to see what this means and to begin to live it. They are only the beginning, a first step.

2.  God is at work in the seminars. They are a chance to respond to God himself.

80

3. Individual sharings:
   — share what made you decide to join the seminars.
   — share what happened to you during the seminars. (how you came to know Christ and be baptized in the Spirit; concrete changes you experienced during that time, e.g. experiencing God's presence, peace, joy, scripture coming alive, and new ability to pray and praise God).
   — share what has happened to you since the seminars (being drawn into Christian community or prayer group, being set free from obstacles, seeing the power of God at work in your life, personal relationships being improved, guidance, teaching).

# SIGN-UP PROCEDURES

It is advisable to have one person in the community or prayer group be responsible for scheduling seminars and for assigning people to the seminars. The longer that person can serve in that position, the more effective he will become at doing it. That person should be at the sign-up session, if possible, but he does not have to be part of the team and come to the team meetings.

The person responsible for scheduling the seminars can often do much of the scheduling during the sharings. People can be told at the end of the session when they can start seminars. When it is not possible to work out the scheduling during the sign-up session or when it is not possible to tell particular individuals when they can start, a letter can be sent to them informing them of the seminar they will be assigned to. It is always good to send a reminder card to all who have signed up, even if they have been told verbally when the seminar begins.

The sign-up cards should ask for basic information (address, phone number, sex, date of birth, marital status, religious affiliation, occupation, if student, whether high school or college, whether already baptized in the Spirit) and should ask if there are any times a person could not attend the seminars. This information can be used not only for assigning people to seminars, but also for preparing the team and the greeters (if greeters are used).

# SEMINAR 1

# God's Love

---

## GOAL

To attract people to the seminar, to dispose them to turn to the Lord, to begin to stir up faith in them.

---

"For God so loved the world that he gave his only son that whoever believes in him should not perish but have eternal life."          (Jn 3:16)

The first seminar is the seminar in which we reach out to people and begin to get to know them. It is a seminar of hope, of promise. In it we speak to people in a simple way about what God is offering to them. We share with them about his love for them, the love which makes him reach out to them and offer them a personal relationship with him. Because he loves them, he wants them to be with him. Because he wants them to be with him and to live in a close, personal friendship with him, he is offering them a new life in the Holy Spirit. God loves us so much that he sent his only son into the world to give us new life and he sent his Spirit to dwell within us so that we might be more closely united to him than we are to anyone or anything else.

The first seminar is not meant to be a time for much instruction. It is an introduction, a seminar of encouragement. The presentation should be short (between 10 and 15 minutes) and it should encourage people to have faith that God will do something significant in the next seven weeks for each of them. The discussion is a time of personal sharing in which we get to know the people better and share with them the things God has done for us. We do not try to accomplish too much in the first seminar: we only try to begin the seminar in such a way that people will want to come back and will want to turn to the Lord. We try to stir up in them a desire for God and a new faith in the Lord.

# The First Team Meeting

1.  Discuss the Life in the Spirit Seminars as a whole (see pp. 8-15)
2.  Discuss the team members' role in the seminars (see pp. 16-21, pp. 24-26)
3.  Preview the first session
    - understand the goal to be achieved
    - go over the format
4.  Go over the discussion groups
5.  Discuss the role of the team member in the first session
    - be in the room before the people come in
    - be warm and friendly; introduce yourself
    - get to know the people and remember their names
    - stay around afterwards to talk and to get to know the people
6.  Pray for the seminars and those who will come to them

# The First Seminar

A.  **Preliminaries**
    1.  The team meets the new people
    2.  Get names, addresses and phone numbers
    3.  If it's a small seminar, have people introduce themselves

B.  **The Team Leader's Presentation Of The Seminar**
    **Introduction:**
    - explain the Life in the Spirit Seminars
    - urge people to come to all of them

1. God is not someone who is beyond our contact, but someone who loves us and wants to be in a personal relationship with us, someone who wants to give us a better life.
2. In the Life in the Spirit Seminars you can take the steps which will allow Jesus Christ to establish or restore or deepen a relationship with you.
3. You can begin right away to turn to the Lord. (Recommend prayer, scripture reading, other reading)
   — distribute *Finding New Life in the Spirit*

C. The Discussion Groups

1. The team leader or assistant divides the seminar into discussion groups and tells them who their discussion leaders are (explaining that the discussion leaders are members of the community).
2. The discussion leader has the group introduce themselves and give a brief background.
3. Discussion starter: Share how you first came to the meeting (the community) and what made you decide to come to the Life in the Spirit Seminars.
4. The discussion leader begins the sharing, including his own religious background, conversion experience(s), and a brief testimony to what the Lord has done for him. If someone in the group does not share important information (like religious background), the discussion leader asks about it in a relaxed, friendly way.
5. The team leader brings the discussion period to a close by leading the whole group in a short prayer and tells them where and when to meet next week.

# COMMENTS ON THE DYNAMICS

Above all else, we have to be welcoming in the first session. We have to make the new people feel at ease. We have to show them that we love them and will be at their disposal. If they can sense that we are there to be their servants and not to be their lords, they will feel much freer to return. As Paul says in Colossians, "Conduct yourselves wisely towards outsiders, making the most of the time. Let your speech always be gracious, seasoned with salt, so that you may know how you ought to answer to everyone" (Col. 4:5-6). In the first seminar, we are dealing with "outsiders" who are interested in becoming "insiders." We have to realize that many of them are not "insiders" yet, but on the other hand, that they soon will be. We should speak to them in a way that will win them, but we should also speak to them in such a way that we are beginning to welcome them as brothers and sisters.

The purpose of the first discussion is to lead the people into a personal sharing of where they are in relation with the Lord. This will allow the team to get to know them better so that they can give them more help. It will particularly help them in reshuffling the discussion groups for next week. The sharing, however, will also introduce the people to one another as people. It will take the seminar out of a theoretical level on to a personal level. Finally, it will give the discussion leader a chance to share what the Lord has done with him, adding one more testimony to the session.

Normally the best way to choose the discussion groups is for the team leader to ask someone to take the list or the file cards people have filled out and to group them in a way which will make the best discussion groups (see p. 38). This will not be the final grouping but the closer it is to the final grouping the better. The assistant can then read out the list after the leader has finished the presentation.

People who are new in the seminars appreciate

receiving clear instructions about what to do. If we try too hard to be nice and end up being vague or hesitant, we do them no service. If we want them to do something (like form a circle for discussion group or share in a personal way in the discussion group) we should say so, gently but firmly, with confidence that what we are saying is best for them.

We should try not to go on too long the first week. We should tell people the time and place where we will begin next week and tell them how long the session will be so they can know what to count on.

If we see people in the seminar who should not become a regular part of the seminar (perhaps they are from out of town), we should explain to them that night why the seminar is not the best place for them and try to help them find the place that will be best for them. Sometimes we can get together with them at another time and talk with them. (Cf. pp. 48-49)

Sometimes we will want to wait another week and collect more people for the seminar. If so, we should explain that to the people who come. We might want to give them a short version of the initial presentation and talk with them and share with them for a short time.

# Expanded Outline of the Presentation

**Introduction**

The team leader introduces himself (if he has not done so before). The Life in the Spirit Seminars are a means to a better life through Christ:

— they last seven weeks in all

— it is important to attend every session

— each seminar brings out part of the whole picture

— (if someone cannot make a seminar for some unavoidable reason, please tell me ahead of time and we'll arrange a way for you to make it up)

I. **God is not beyond our contact, but someone who loves us and wants to be in a personal relationship with us, and who wants to give us a better life.**

A. Our misconceptions of Christianity can be an obstacle to our finding this better life through Christ:

1. Christianity as a restrictive morality (Christianity as rules to keep so we can go to heaven);
2. Christianity only as loving your neighbor ("as long as I live a good life it doesn't matter what I believe");
3. God as someone whom we can not contact, who does not do anything that we can experience or know to be his work.

B. The truth is:

— God loves us;

- he wants to make contact with us and have a personal relationship with us;
- he wants to give us a new and better life;
- for this reason, he sent his only Son, Jesus.

C. We can experience a better life as a result of authentic Christianity:
- the knowledge of God and the power to live the Christian life;
- happiness; peace and joy; better personal relationships; healing;
- genuine community

II. In the Life in the Spirit Seminars, you can take steps which will allow Jesus Christ to establish or restore or deepen a relationship with you.

A. Everyone can experience a change:

1. Those who have been merely nominal Catholics or fallen-away Catholics: during the next seven weeks, Jesus will offer you a whole new life — you can find or recover a genuine relationship with him (be baptized in the Spirit and experience spiritual gifts).

2. Those who have been trying to live the Christian life in some way but who have found it difficult or who have not experienced much contact with God: during the next seven weeks, Jesus will give you an experiential contact with him so that you will know that you know him, and he will give you new power to live the Christian life (he will baptize you in the Spirit, let you experience spiritual gifts).

3. For Catholics who have already experienced

personal contact with Christ, during the next seven weeks, Jesus will give you a new and fuller relationship with himself (prayer "in the Spirit", spiritual gifts).

4. For those of you who have already been baptized in the Spirit, the Lord will teach you more during this time about what it means to be baptized in the Spirit and he will lead you into a deeper life in the Spirit.

B. But the Life in the Spirit Seminars are only the beginning:

1. To experience the better life Christ offers, you need to grow to maturity in your relationship with him.

2. In the next three weeks we will help you to understand and take the first steps
   — in the last two weeks, we will explain to you how to go on
   — after that, there are other opportunities and helps which will make it possible for you to grow in what you have begun here.

3. In the next week or so, a greeter from the community (prayer group) will call on you and help you make better contact with the life of the community (prayer group).
   — one of the most important ways to learn about Christianity is to see how others live it.

III. You can begin right away to turn to the Lord

A. The Lord will reach out to you, but you must reach out to him.
"When you call to me and come to me, I will listen to you. When you seek me, you shall find me." (Jer. 29:12-13)

B.  Starting tonight:
— pray every day to the Lord
— meditate on his words (explain how to use
*Finding New Life in the Spirit*)
— if you can, read. . .

# COMMENTS ON THE PRESENTATION

(Introduction) At the beginning we must emphasize the importance of each session of the seminars. We need not fear that we shall discourage people by telling them to attend every week; rather, if we speak to them gently but firmly, we will impress upon them the seriousness and importance of the step they are taking.

(I) The first section is best presented in the form of a brief personal testimony. We want to assure people who have had bad or inadequate experiences with Christianity that they can expect to find something different here; we want to assure them that they can and will have a better life through what Jesus will do for them. One of the best ways to communicate all of this is to tell them how these very things happened in our own lives.

The speaker should keep in mind that if he is going to give the presentation in seminar 3, he will have to give another personal testimony to what it means to be baptized in the Spirit. The two testimonies should be somewhat different. This first personal testimony should center mainly on turning to the Lord and the difference the Lord has made in the speaker's life. It should emphasize the fact that we can actually know God personally, by experience and not just by hearsay. The second testimony will center more on being baptized in the Spirit and the changes that come through the new relationship with the Holy Spirit.

In this edition of the Manual, the assumption is that most or all of the people in the seminars will come from a Catholic background. For many, their experience of the church was negative or inadequate. Many will have experienced either a traditional form of church life with a strong emphasis on rigid rules and arbitrary practices or a more contemporary, "secularized" Christianity which stressed loving other people, but downplayed or ignored a personal relationship with Jesus Christ. Neither form of Christianity gives the kind of life which God wants to offer people. Both forms of Christianity make God seem distant. We must remember, however, that there is also a good deal of authentic Christianity around. When we talk about misconceptions of Christianity or the bad experiences which people may have had, we do not want to give the impression that we think that everyone has misconceptions or has had bad experiences. Our only purpose is to assure those who have been "turned off" to Christianity by past experiences that they will find something different in the Life in the Spirit Seminars.

(II) In the second section, we want to make a simple point: Jesus will do something for us in the seminar. We can expect something to happen to us. He will use the seminar to establish or restore or deepen in us a relationship with himself. But on the other hand, the seminar will be just the beginning of a new life. In order to go on after the seminar, we will need further help.

The purpose of going through the four categories of people is to explain to people in concrete terms what might happen to them. Everyone who has not been baptized in the Spirit can be baptized in the Spirit, but this will mean a different change for different people. For some it will mean coming out of a situation in which their Catholicism is purely nominal to a situation in which they can live the life of the Spirit. These people will experience the biggest change. For some, it will mean the addition of an experiential dimension to their Christian life. They will come to know the Lord and see him work in their lives. Those people who already know the Lord and know his power can enter into a new "charismatic dimension", and can experience the Lord in a new and more powerful way. Finally, any people in the seminar who have already been baptized in the Spirit will find further help in the instruction and experience of the seminar.

(II.B.3) This section is only to be used by prayer groups or communities that have a "greeter" system. See Part III of this manual.

(III) The final section is a short exhortation to turn to the Lord daily. In it we share advice on the importance of prayer, meditation, and reading. Telling the people in the seminar what they can do to cooperate with the seminar will make it much easier for them to open up to the Lord.

### HELPFUL MATERIALS

Some passages which might be used in the talk to support what the speaker is saying: Jn 3:16, Jn 1:12, Jn 10:10b, Jn 14:23, Rev 3:20, Isa 45:18-19, Ezek 34:15-16, Ps 145:18.

Background reading for the speaker: Stephen Clark's *Baptized in the Spirit and Spiritual Gifts.*

# SEMINAR 2

# Salvation

---

## GOAL

To help people see the momentousness of Christianity, to help them understand the basic Christian message (what Jesus has done and will do for them), to help them realize the need to make a serious decision.

---

"He has delivered us from the dominion of darkness and transferred us to the kingdom of his beloved son."     (Col 1:13)

The second seminar is the seminar in which people can come to see the full dimensions of Christianity. In it we present the vision that is contained in the message of the good news about Jesus. It is the seminar in which people are presented with the reality of the two kingdoms (two ways of life, two societies) in the world, and have to face the question whether their lives reflect life in the kingdom of Christ or not. This is the time when people should realize that they are not just getting a "blessing" when they are baptized in the Spirit, but they are committing themselves to a total reorientation of life.

Those people who come to the second seminar are beginning to be in earnest. They have made a fairly definite decision to stick with the seminars, usually because they want the new life that is being offered. The message of the talk is a sobering one. Interest and curiosity characterized the first week; growing seriousness characterizes the second week.

# The Second Team Meeting

1.  Review last week's seminar
    - discuss any problems that appeared and what to do about them
    - go over the list of people and consider what should be done for each one
    - work out the final discussion groups
2.  Preview the second seminar
    - understand the goal to be achieved
    - go over the format and the talk
3.  Discuss what the team member should do
    - the need to still be welcoming and to get to know people in the seminar
    - go over the discussion and discussion question, being clear on what the discussion should accomplish
4.  Pray for the seminar and those in it

# The Second Seminar

A.  **The talk**
1.  There is something seriously wrong with the world (with society as a whole and with individual lives) — something major is needed.
2.  Since the cause of what is wrong with society is something bigger than man can handle on his own (Satan, sin, and the dominion of darkness), men need God to find the new life they want.

3. God sent Jesus, his son, to break the hold of Satan and give us new life through his death and resurrection. Jesus is the Lord and Savior.

Recommend reading and encourage them to continue turning to the Lord. Encourage them to come on time, if necessary.

B.   The Discussion Group

Discussion starter: What things make you most feel the need for Christ? Provide an opportunity sometime in the discussion for those in the group to ask any questions or discuss the things on their minds.

# COMMENTS ON THE DYNAMICS

Much of what is true for the first seminar is also true for the second seminar. From the point of view of the way people feel, the second seminar is still introductory. The team has to be welcoming. By the end of this seminar, each discussion leader should know who the people in his discussion group are, and he should know something about them, especially where they are in relationship to the Lord and the seminars.

# Expanded Outline of the Presentation

I.   There is something seriously wrong with the world (with society as a whole and with individual lives) — something major is needed.

   A.   God made the world to be a place of peace and justice and happiness, a place in which he would reign. He still wants the world to be that way. (Isa 2:1-5).

   B.   But everyone agrees that there is something seriously wrong with the way the world is now (war, poverty, riots, racial conflict, generation gap, exploitation).

   C.   There is a growing realization that there is more than just a number of individual problems — society as a whole, the system as a whole, has something wrong with it (where is it all going? social problems getting worse, no one on top of the situation, technology and social change out of men's control).

   D.   Individuals suffer from the situation and from lack of help, and they experience many problems (loneliness, isolation, depression, anxieties, insecurities, lack of direction, meaninglessness; personal relationships characterized by fear, suspicion, mistrust, exploitation).

   E.   Something major is needed to correct the situation in the world.

II.  Since the cause of what is wrong with society is something bigger than man can handle on his own

(Satan, sin, and the dominion of darkness), men
need God to find the new life they want.

A.   Men make various efforts to improve the world:
1. There are a variety of secular efforts, but they
   are not succeeding
      — even the most educated men in our
        universities are having a hard time
        making a go of their own lives, work,
        and relationships
      — even the most highly placed executives
        in our modern business corporations
        are having a hard time making a go
        of their own lives, work, and rela-
        tionships
2. Religions which men have developed try to
   achieve a solution:  Buddhism, yoga, tran-
   scendental meditation, etc.
3. Some forms of Christianity amount to being
   man's efforts to find a good life and change
   the world:  secular Christianity, types of
   traditionalist Christianity.

But these are all based on man's wisdom; God's
wisdom is needed (Isa 55: 8-9).

B.   God tells us that:
1. We are not just confronted with particular
   wrongs in society or in ourselves; behind
   the particular things that are wrong there
   is something bigger than most men can
   handle:
      — the pervasive power of sin (Rom 3:9,
        23)
      — a kingdom, the dominion of darkness
        (Col 1:13)
      — a force in rebellion against God, at
        enmity with him (Eph 6: 12)

100

        — Satan is behind it (I Jn 5:19)

        — we are not free, nor is our society (people are in spiritual bondage, under the oppression of evil) (Eph 2:1-3)

2. Man was created to need God to achieve true peace, justice, and truth:

        — the spiritual realm is not an optional extra (Jn 15:5c)

        — only in God's kingdom (under his rule) are these things possible (Isa 2:1-5, Isa 45:22)

        — under God's rule, life can be changed now (Isa 48:17-18, Mk 1:14-15)

3. There is a choice before us: to live under the dominion of darkness or in the kingdom of God.

III. **God sent his son Jesus to break the hold of Satan and give us new life through his death and resurrection. Jesus is the Lord and Savior.**

  A. God sent his son to free us from darkness and Satan. Jesus is the Christ (the messiah, the one God sent) (Col 1:13, Jn 11:21-27, Mt 16:13-17).

  B. Jesus died for our sins and rose to give us new life (Rom 4:25, Col 1:20, Tit 3:3-7):

        — if he had not died, we would not have been freed from our sins (Isa 53:4-6, Heb 9:11-28)

        — he broke the hold of Satan (Jn 12:31, I Jn 4:4)

        — salvation is more than just going to heaven: it is a whole new way of life on earth as well (Jn 10: 10b, Jn 4:14).

**C.** Jesus is Lord (God gave full power and authority to Jesus to bring freedom and new life to those who accept him) (Mt 28:18, Phil 2:5-11). Jesus lives in his church and acts through it and in it to bring life to those who are his followers (Eph. 2:17-22).

**D.** Next week: we will discuss what the new life is and what a person can expect from being baptized in the Spirit.

# COMMENTS ON THE PRESENTATION

The second talk is on "salvation." "Salvation" means "God saves us." When we talk about salvation, we talk about what God has done, is doing, and will do to save us. Our usual concept of salvation is limited to the ideas of the forgiveness of our sins and our admission into heaven. Sometimes it will also include a personal knowledge of Christ. While all these things (forgiveness of sins, admission to heaven, knowledge of Christ) are important parts of salvation, the fullness of God's salvation exceeds even these. God is at work in Christ to bring us to a full life on earth, a life that involves peace and happiness, freedom from sin and Satan, healing, and spiritual power. Even more, God is at work to bring a new kingdom, and he has sent Christ, who has intended the church to be a new people, a society where people live under the reign of God and are free from the rule of Satan. Salvation is not just something for the future, it is now. Salvation is not just something that brings me a personal good, it brings a whole new life in a new society.

The purpose of this second talk is to make people realize how big a thing Christianity is. In some ways the talk is a test of faith for the speaker. He is called upon to make a proclamation of faith, to say something that those who are listening to him have not experienced and cannot experience for a while. He is called, in short, to proclaim the gospel. He cannot justify what he says other than by saying: this is what God has told us. He simply has to rely on the fact that God has revealed to us that there is more going on in the world than unaided human eyes can see. Men are in the middle of spiritual realities, both hellish and heavenly. It is not until they can see with eyes of faith thay they can begin to understand what is happening to them.

(I) The first section of the talk is meant to describe the situation in the world as most people can see it. We do not have to say that everything is wrong with the world. All we are saying is that there is something that is wrong with the world, and that it is something serious, in fact, major. There will be few people in the seminar who will not agree with this.

The first section can be presented in a brief, straight-forward way, just as it is outlined in the presentation. There is no need to offer proof that there is something wrong with the world, we can simply state it as an obvious fact. It helps to tell some personal stories of experiences that helped us realize the condition of the world.

(II) The second section is far from being obvious. In fact, it can only be learned by God's revelation. We make a mistake if we try to prove it; we can only say, "God said so". That is the reason why there are so many scripture passages indicated in the extended outline. The speaker will not want to use every one of those passages, but he will want to know where "God said so".

(II.B.1.) The section on sin, Satan, and the dominion of darkness can be difficult for people to give. In fact, the degree to which we have personally experienced God's salvation will affect our ability to speak this message in faith. If we have not yet experienced freedom from the power of Satan, if our life is not yet so different from the lives of those around us, we cannot speak these words in the same kind of faith and conviction that we have when we have seen such changes. We should rely on the Lord to lead us in how we personally should make this point.

In preparing for this talk, the speaker can read Michael Harper's *Spiritual Warfare* and Watchman Nee's *Love Not the World*. Both present the cosmic view of salvation which the talk needs. Both help to place us in contact with spiritual realities. He might also consider the meditation on the two standards in the second week of the *Spiritual Exercises* of St. Ignatius.

When we come to the point of speaking about Satan and the dominion of darkness, we should present the truth simply and powerfully. We often think that modern men are unwilling to accept the existence of Satan. It is certainly true that some people are, and some of those people may be in our seminar. But most modern men have actually suspected for a long time that Satan exists and is at work. Many have had experiences of encountering evil spirits, or at least of suspecting that that is what they were encountering.

When we talk about the kingdom of Satan, we can call people's attention to a few simple facts. We can say, "Most of us have felt that what is wrong with the world is something that is bigger than we are, something, in fact, that is bigger than the sum total of what individual men have done wrong. We have felt that there was some force behind it." We can also say, "Many of you have had experiences of sensing the existence of evil powers." We can rely on the Lord to bring home the truth of these statements.

(II.B.3) At the end of section II, the people in the seminar should see that they need help and that they need to make a big choice. What the choice involves will not be too concrete to them at this point. All they need to know is that in choosing Jesus and the life of the Spirit they are choosing something bigger than a personal blessing.

(III) The final section is simply stating the good news of Jesus. God has become man in Jesus. Jesus is the Lord. He died for our sins and rose again.

(III.B) There is a temptation Christians sometimes face. In the attempt to have Christianity make sense to non-Christians, they talk about Jesus in a way that avoids the "foolishness of the cross". Paul said that "the work of the cross is folly to those who are perishing, but to us who are being saved it is the power of God." (I Cor 1:18). We cannot make complete sense of the cross in humanly understandable terms. But that does not mean we should avoid it. We were saved because Jesus died on the cross, because he shed his blood for us. He was the sacrifice for our sins. If he had not died and risen again, we would not have experienced salvation. All we can do is to tell the facts. Jesus' death and resurrection saved us. We who have experienced the power of the cross should not be ashamed to tell men that it is through the cross that they can be saved. As Paul said, "For the Jews demand signs and the Greeks seek wisdom, but we preach Christ crucified, a stumbling block to the Jews and folly to the Gentiles, but to those who are called, both Jews and Greeks, Christ the power of God and the wisdom of God is stronger than men." (I Cor 1:22-25)

(General) The talk as a whole can be dry if it is not well prepared. In general, the message should be presented simply, without a lot of elaboration or explanation. Different anecdotes and stories can be used to enliven the presentation. Some scripture is essential to back up the points.

# SEMINAR 3

# The New Life

---

## GOAL

To witness to the fact that the good news is indeed good news, to let the people know that a new life is available through (a fuller) reception of the Holy Spirit, to help them to see that this new life centers in an experiential relationship with the Lord.

---

"I came so that they may have life and have it in abundance."   (Jn 10:10)

The third seminar is a very personal seminar. It is the seminar in which we center on the new life that each person can have. It is the seminar in which we explain to people what it means to be baptized in the Spirit. It is probably here that the most people turn to Christ in a new way, because they can see in concrete terms the kind of personal changes that are being offered to them.

The heart of this seminar is the personal testimony.

The speaker should make the bulk of his presentation a personal testimony of how he came to be baptized in the Spirit and the difference it made in his life. The personal testimony can make a powerful change in people's attitudes. It can also be the most effective teaching method. People can receive a lot of theory about what it means to be baptized in the Spirit, but when they can hear a story of what happened to someone when he was baptized in the Spirit, they really begin to understand what the baptism in the Spirit is.

# The Third Team Meeting

**The third team meeting**

1.  Review last week's seminar
    - discuss any problems that appeared and what to do about them
    - go over the list of people and consider what should be done for them

2.  Preview the third seminar
    - understand the goal to be achieved
    - go over the discussion and the discussion question, being clear on what the discussion should accomplish

3.  Discuss the personal contact to be made after the fourth seminar
    - when a person is ready to be baptized in the Spirit
    - how to talk with him to discover if he is ready
    - what he thinks baptism in the Spirit is; what he thinks the gift of tongues is
    - whether he has repented of serious sin
    - what he thinks will happen to him when he is prayed with
    - the need to make an appointment with each person in the seminar this week for the week after the fourth seminar

4.  Pray for the seminar and for those in it

# The Third Seminar

A. **The Talk**

1. The Father wants all men to have new life. He sent his son Jesus into the world so that we could be given the source of new life, the Holy Spirit.

2. When the Holy Spirit comes to a person, he becomes a changed man; he is given the power to know God and to live a new life. (Include personal testimony here.)

3. There is no need for anyone to be the kind of Christian who is not in vital contact with God or who does not experience the power of the Holy Spirit in his life.

   —everyone, even beginners in the Christian life, can be baptized in the Spirit.

4. Baptism in the Spirit is only the beginning of a new life.

Inform them about being prayed with in two weeks and about meeting with their discussion leader to talk about it during the week before they are prayed with.

B. **The Discussion Group**

1. Discussion starters: Do you understand what it means to be baptized in the Spirit? Do you understand what the gift of tongues is and why someone would want to pray in tongues?

2. After the discussion group, make an appointment with each person to meet during the week after the next seminar.

## COMMENTS ON THE DYNAMICS

There is usually a change in people in the third seminar. Most people are affected by the talk. A new faith and a new desire to change are coming to birth in their hearts. The role of the team is to foster that new faith and new desire.

Discussion starters may not be needed for the discussion this week or the weeks after. Frequently the discussion group is ready to get right into discussion after the talk. However, some discussion groups may always need discussion starters.

(The contact after the fourth week) It is essential to get together with each person during the week before praying with him to be baptized in the Spirit. This personal contact serves a number of functions:

1) It allows us to answer the questions and problems people still have about being baptized in the Spirit. Most often they are questions which the person did not feel free to ask in a larger group. Sometimes the questions have already been discussed in the discussion group, but this person needs to be reassured about them.

2) The personal contact can also give people the encouragement and faith they need in order to pray with faith to be baptized in the Spirit. Their natural fears and hesitations, and also Satan, are at work to keep them from placing their trust in God. During the course of the personal contact the team member should try to show the person which of his fears are natural and which may be temptations from the evil one.

3) The personal contact is also a time to talk in greater depth about the gifts of the Spirit, especially tongues. During this contact, we can provide some help in yielding to tongues.

4) The personal contact is a time to tell those whom you feel are not ready to be prayed with to be baptized in the Spirit that they should wait for a while. The most common reasons are that they have not

yet decided to repent of serious sin or make a commitment to the Lord and that they have not come to believe that the Lord will do anything for them. Sometimes people who are excessively fearful can be helped by a wait of another week; the experience of seeing people be prayed with often allays their fears. Sometimes we can suggest to these people that we will pray with them for greater faith in the fifth week of the seminar, and then pray with them to be baptized in the Spirit the following week (sometimes they will be baptized in the Spirit as they pray for greater faith).

It is good to have the commitment forms (section B of the expanded outline of Seminar #5) mimeographed and given to the people in the seminar on the fourth week. In the personal contact, we can take a copy and ask them if they are ready to make this commitment. Reviewing the commitment form with them will often reveal some difficulties.

We make the appointment this week to insure that the person will be available during the week prior to the fifth seminar. For most people, a week and a half is enough notice, but only a half a week may not be. We should make sure that they know that we will not pray with them without having met once with them individually.

(Special prayer) It is possible to pray over people for a growth in faith and commitment to the Lord before the fifth week. Whenever we discern that someone in the discussion group needs help and feel that he will be open to being prayed with, we can pray with him after the seminar. Such prayer will often make a big difference for him.

It is not uncommon for people to be baptized in the Spirit on their own, without being prayed with. As they grow in faith, this can happen at any time, and after the third seminar it becomes somewhat common. We should not be uneasy if it does happen, nor should we encourage it to happen. Most people will make a firmer commitment to Christ and better repentance if they are not baptized in the Spirit until they have made some clear decisions about their life.

# Expanded Outline of the Presentation

I.  The Father wants all men to have new life. He sent his son Jesus into the world so that we could be given the source of new life, the Holy Spirit.

   A.  Often the Christianity which we have come in contact with has not been spiritually alive, but today God is renewing his Church by a fresh outpouring of his Spirit.

   B.  The Father wants all men to have new life in him.

   C.  The Father sent his son into the world to bring us new life:

      1.  Jesus is Lord; if we accept his lordship, we can experience a new freedom and a new life.

      2.  In him all our sins can be forgiven (no matter what we have done), and every barrier between us and the Father can be taken away.

      3.  After Jesus rose from the dead and ascended to the Father, he sent the Holy Spirit to bring us new life (Acts 1:1-5).

II.  When the Holy Spirit comes to someone, he becomes a changed man (Acts 2 or Acts 19:1-7).

   A.  He comes to know God by experience:

      — he comes to know God as his Father who loves him and cares for him

      — he experiences God's love and presence in a new way

      — he experiences God speaking in his heart, teaching him, guiding him

      — he comes to know Jesus as his Lord

      — the lordship of Jesus begins to be the basic principle for his way of life

B.   He can pray in a new way:
— his prayer becomes more centered on God,
  less on himself
— his prayer is more often prayer of praise and
  thanksgiving
— he discovers that he can pray in tongues; the
  gift of tongues is:
  — a means of spiritual growth
  — prayer the Spirit inspires within us to
    praise God
  — prayer the Spirit inspires within us when
    we cannot pray adequately
C.   The Bible, the liturgy, the sacraments come to life.
D.   The fruit of the Spirit develops within him (love,
  joy, peace, etc. — Gal 5).
E.   He can receive the gifts of the Spirit to serve God
  (prophecy, healing, discernment of spirits,
  inspirations to speak — I Cor 12).

III.   **Full life in the Spirit begins when we are baptized in
  the Spirit. Being baptized in the Spirit allows us to
  experience fuller life in the Spirit.**
A.   When we are baptized in the Spirit, the Holy Spirit
  comes to us in such a way that we can experience his presence and see it change us.
— this is not our first reception of the Holy
  Spirit, but a release of his power that is
  already within us through baptism and
  confirmation.
B.   Different people see different changes happen to
  them as a result of being baptized in the Spirit.
1. Many may consciously experience the Holy
  Spirit in them for the first time. Others who
  have already consciously experienced something of the Spirit's presence in their lives
  can receive a fuller experience, may become

114

aware of new effects, new changes which the Spirit brings about in them. Everyone can experience a new presence and working of the Spirit.

2. Those of us who have been Christians before will see that our years of Christian living have provided us with many resources that will be brought to life by the new presence of the Spirit in us.

C.  No Christian should lack contact with God or be powerless as a Christian.

— everyone, even beginners in the Christian life, can be baptized in the Spirit.

IV.  Baptism in the Spirit is only the beginning of a new life.

A.  With the help of committed Christians as our brothers and sisters, we can grow to spiritual maturity.

B.  We can develop a daily communion and friendship with Christ.

C.  We can experience a new peace and joy, see ourselves being healed, becoming loving people.

D.  We can develop better relationships.

Next week: we will discuss how to turn to Christ so that we can receive the fullness of the new life he is offering.

The week after: there will be an opportunity to receive prayer to be baptized in the Spirit.

We would like to have you talk with your discussion leader during the week before you are prayed with (not this week but the next one), and we would like to ask you to make an appointment with him tonight after the discussion group.

If you are interested in learning more about spiritual gifts, we would like to recommend that you read the pamphlet

*Baptized in the Spirit and Spiritual Gifts.* If you are interested in a fuller presentation of the relationship between being baptized in the Spirit and the sacraments, we would like to recommend that you read the pamphlet *Confirmation and the Baptism in the Holy Spirit.*

# COMMENTS ON THE PRESENTATION

(Explaining baptism in the Spirit): There are many ways of explaining what it means to be baptized in the Spirit among Christians today. Some of them were developed by people who do not believe that the Holy Spirit is given in baptism and confirmation. The way some people present the meaning of being baptized in the Spirit gives the impression that everyone needs the experience of being baptized in the Spirit in order to have the Holy Spirit at all. Such a view is incompatible with the Catholic understanding of the sacraments of initiation. Moreover, it puts so great an emphasis on the conscious experience of the presence of the Holy Spirit that the experience becomes the sole criterion by which a person can know whether he has received the Holy Spirit or not.

Catholics do not accept the view that conscious experience is the sole criterion of the presence of the Spirit in a person; on the other hand, neither would it be according to genuine Catholic tradition to think that it is a matter of indifference whether a Christian experiences anything of the power of the Spirit in his life or not.

The dominant view of the baptism in the Holy Spirit is one found in the first Malines Document, *Theological and Pastoral Orientations on the Catholic Charismatic Renewal* (pp. 29-33). This is the view which we present here. There are, however, other ways of understanding this working of the Holy Spirit, many of which contain valuable insights. For an able exposition of one such view, see "Baptism in the Holy Spirit: A Catholic Interpretation of the Pentecostal Experience," by Francis A. Sullivan, S.J. in *Gregorianum,* Vol. 55-fasc. 1 (1974), Rome: Gregorian University Press.

Catholics will see being baptized in the Spirit as a release of what has already been given in baptism and confirmation. Praying over people is not a sacramental action (at least, certainly not in the full theological sense of sacramental action). It is rather a way of bringing people to a release of faith where they appropriate fully what has been given to them and so experience its full effect. Hence, being baptized in the Spirit can be seen as a renewal of the sacraments of initiation.

Terminology is problematic in this area. Most of the terms for this release of the Spirit that are commonly used ("baptized in the Spirit," "outpouring of the Spirit") refer in Scripture to the initial gift of the Spirit at the point of Christian initiation. Hence they easily lead to confusion. On the other hand, in many countries, "baptism in the Spirit" is so commonly used that it does not seem that it can be replaced. It has, moreover, the advantage that most Catholics have never heard the term before, and hence they do not readily confuse it with the gift of the Spirit in Christian initiation. Whatever term is used, the explanation given is very important. For example, if we use the phrase, "baptism in the Spirit," we should avoid the idea that sacramental baptism is only baptism in water. If the term, "outpouring" is used, we should take care not to leave the impression that there is no outpouring of the Spirit which takes place in sacramental baptism. What we are speaking of is not the initial gift of the Spirit to Christians, but a release of that gift so that the presence of the Holy Spirit in them comes to conscious experience and the power of the Holy Spirit begins to take effect experientially in their lives. In countries where "being baptized in the Spirit" or "baptism in the Spirit" is the normal term, the speakers in the seminar should explain that what they are talking about is the same thing that people mean when they speak or write about being baptized in the Spirit, especially since this term has been so widely used in the renewal.

There is likewise a possible danger of confusion when New Testament texts on the reception of the Holy Spirit are used in the seminars. Texts which describe the effects of the initial gift of the Spirit (e.g. that by the gift of the Spirit we are made adopted sons of God) cannot be applied without explanation to the effects of the release of the Spirit in a Catholic who is already baptized and confirmed.

On the other hand, we must keep in mind that the experience of already baptized and confirmed Catholics today when they are baptized in the Spirit is often very similar to the experience of people described in the New Testament at the moment of their initial reception of the Holy Spirit (cf. Acts 2:8, 10-11, 19). In a way similar to that depicted in the New Testament, many Catholics today enter into experiential contact with God for the first time when they are baptized in the Spirit. Likewise, many of them experience such manifestations of the Spirit's presence as peace, joy, fervor, and charismatic gifts.

The New Testament texts are important, both because they state the promises on which every further release of the Spirit is based and because they show that the gift of the Holy Spirit in the Christian can and should be consciously experienced. The speaker, therefore, should use those texts carefully, and at the appropriate point in the seminar (IIIA above) should explain the relationship of baptism in the Spirit to the sacraments of initiation.

While doctrinal clarity is important, it would be a mistake to focus on doctrinal questions more than is necessary. The goal is to bring people to a new faith in the presence of the Holy Spirit in their lives and an ability to actively "reach out" to receive what God wants to do in them. We should therefore talk mainly about the Holy Spirit himself and what he does in the lives of believers. If people can see what is promised in the gift of the Spirit, they will discover for themselves what is missing in their lives. If they see something is missing, they will be ready for a change. Personal testimony is very important in this process. The speaker should explain what has happened to normal, contemporary human beings. If people can see that something has happened to people like themselves that has not yet happened to them, they will begin to develop a hunger to have the same thing themselves.

The way we talk about being baptized in the Spirit can make a big difference in how people approach it. Often we can talk about it as being something important in itself. We can emphasize the fact that it is a special experience that we can "get". Or we can talk about people who "got it" and people who have not yet "got it". Instead, we should center our concern upon the Holy Spirit and upon the new life we can have through a new relationship with him. Being baptized in the Spirit only means being introduced to an experiential relationship with the Holy Spirit. It is meant to be the beginning of a new kind of life lived in a fuller power of God. Someone who has been baptized in the Spirit and who does not go on to live in the Spirit is probably not much better off than someone who has not been baptized in the Spirit and does not live in the Spirit. Living in the Spirit has to be the center of our concern, not being baptized in the Spirit.

In order to avoid thinking of being baptized in the Spirit as an "it," a thing in itself, it is better to avoid using the phrase "the baptism in the Spirit." It is better to speak of being baptized in the Spirit. We do not receive the baptism in the Holy Spirit (scripture never speaks that way). We enter into a new relationship with the Holy Spirit. We do not get a thing called the baptism in the Spirit that we get to keep all our lives. When we are baptized in the Spirit we do not "get" anything. Rather we enter into a new relationship with the Spirit of God.

(I) The first section of the talk is meant to be a brief introduction. Its purpose is to recall the offer of new life that has been spoken about before in the seminars and to connect that offer of new life with the Holy Spirit. We can have new life because the Holy Spirit is given to us. The purpose of the introduction is also to recall that it is Jesus who gives us this new life. Jesus is the baptizer in the Holy Spirit. He makes it all possible.

(II) This section presents the scriptural account of what happens to a person when he receives the gift of the Holy Spirit. The next section talks about the release of the Spirit through being baptized in the Spirit.

Section II is also meant to be the outline for a personal testimony. In it the speaker shares what has happened to him. In the course of the sharing, he can mention how items A-F happened to him.

There are a number of passages in scripture which can be used to introduce the section on what happens to a person when he is baptized in the Spirit. Acts 2, Acts 8, Acts 10-11, and Acts 19 all contain scenes in which people receive the Spirit. Whatever passages are used, the speaker should emphasize one thing: it is the real change that takes place in a person that is the convincing sign that the Holy Spirit is doing something new in him. Such changes are usually such that other people can see that something new is going on in that person's life, and that he is really different. It should not be just a secret, invisible change that no one (the man himself included) knows has happened. The speaker should avoid saying that just because a person has no way of establishing such a statement. All we should say is that when the changes are the kind of things we would expect

God to do, we can rightly conclude that the Holy Spirit is present and working in that person in a new way.

Acts 19:1-7 is a particularly good passage to use. Paul comes to Ephesus and there meets a group of "disciples". He apparently thinks they are Christians, but he senses that there is something wrong. So he asks a question, "Did you receive the Holy Spirit when you believed?" For us, that would be a strange question to ask. Few of us would think of asking whether a person had received the Holy Spirit when he believed if we saw something missing in his Christian life. And if we were asked such a question before being baptized in the Spirit, many of us would not know how to answer. If we had been asked if we had received the Holy Spirit, we would not have known how to tell. And yet Paul apparently expected every Christian to know that they had received the Holy Spirit. He expected a yes or no answer. With the group of disciples in Acts 19, it turned out that his suspicions were confirmed. They had only received. the baptism of John the Baptist and had not been instructed as Christians. Paul completed their initiation into Christ, and when he laid hands on them for the Holy Spirit, something happened to them. They spoke in tongues and prophesied.

(II.C) The main presentation of the gift of tongues should be in the form of a personal testimony. Tongues should be explained as a gift of prayer, usually a gift of praise. Tongues can also be used with interpretation to build up a group of Christians, but we do not want to go into that too much here. What is important for people to understand at this point in the seminar is that tongues can be a great help to their prayer life. Moreover, a short description of what it is like to pray in tongues is very valuable to people at this point.

(II.F) This is the only place in the seminars where the spiritual gifts are spoken about. The presentation could be longer or shorter depending on the need of the people. If we make the presentation short, we will definitely want to recommend reading at the end.

(III) We want to say something simple in this section. We want to say that there is a life in the Spirit which can be experienced, which we can see concrete results from. What happened to the early Christians and what happened to the speaker can happen to us. This life in the Spirit begins when we are baptized in the Spirit, when a change is made in our relationship with the Holy Spirit such that we can begin to experience his presence in a new way. Different Christians are at different points in their relationship with the Holy Spirit. Some have already experienced some of the things which happened to the speaker, but everyone can expect that all the things which come from being baptized in the Spirit (A-F) and are not now part of their lives will become a part of their lives.

(IV) The last section is meant to emphasize the idea that baptism in the Spirit is not an end in itself. It is meant to be the beginning of a new life in the Spirit. We will need help for this new life. We will need to go on, and going on will not be automatic, but it can happen if we want it to.

HELPFUL MATERIALS:

Clark's *Baptized in the Spirit and Spiritual Gifts* is helpful in clearing up questions about what it means to be baptized in the Spirit. Gee's *Concerning Spiritual Gifts* and Christenson's *Speaking in Tongues* are helpful for questions in the area of speaking in tongues and spiritual gifts.

# SEMINAR 4

# Receiving
# God's Gift

---

## GOAL

To help people turn away from everything that is
incompatible with the Christian life and to prepare them to ask in faith for the full life of the
Spirit.

---

"If anyone thirst, let him come to me, and let
him who believes in me drink. As the scripture
has said, 'Out of his heart shall flow rivers of
living water.' "                    (John 7:37-38)

The fourth seminar is the seminar of final preparation.
The message has been spoken. God's promise has been presented. Now is the time for those who are ready to take the
steps of preparation. This is the "how to do it" week.

We should not attempt to do too much in this seminar.
We do not have to present a ringing call to total and complete dedication to Jesus. We do not have to present the demands of absolute discipleship. We do not have to insist on
miracle-working faith. We do not have to urge them to seek

deep spiritual revelations. All we have to do is to help people take some concrete steps that will help them to be baptized in the Spirit. Once they are in a relationship with the Holy Spirit that allows him to work directly in their lives, he can lead into all these things.

# The Fourth Team Meeting

1. Review last week's seminar
   - discuss any problems that appeared and what to do about them
   - go over the list of people and consider what should be done for them
2. Preview the fourth seminar
   - understand the goal to be achieved
   - go over the discussion and the discussion questions, being clear on what the discussion should accomplish
   - arrange to get more people to help with the fifth week, if needed
3. Discuss what is happening to people this week and how to help them with it
   - how to help people repent
   - how to help people have faith
   - consider the different types of people and the special help they need
   - go over briefly the personal contact in the week coming up and stress its importance
4. Pray for the seminar and the people in it

# The Fourth Seminar

A. The Talk
   1. In order to receive the new life God is offering to us, we must turn away from those things which

block our relationship with God and accept Jesus as our Lord.

2. In order to receive the new life God is offering to us, we must ask him for it in faith, expecting to receive it because he wants us to have it and he promised he would give it to us.

3. Next week you will be able to pray with others to be baptized in the Spirit, and when you do, you *will be.*

B. The Discussion Group

1. Discussion starter: What has the Lord taught you so far about what you need to do to repent? What do you expect will happen to you next week? Do you have any questions about the gift of tongues?

2. The discussion leader should begin the discussion by answering the first question and in doing so he should give a short testimony to the way he turned to the Lord and to how he experienced being baptized in the Spirit. He should include a few remarks about the difficulties he may have had in repentance and the fears he may have had before being prayed with to be baptized in the Holy Spirit.

C. Concluding Remarks (by the leader, after the discussions)

Give a brief explanation of the format of seminar #5 and urge them to be faithful to the meeting with their discussion leaders this week and to talk over with them any difficulties.

# COMMENTS ON THE DYNAMICS

From the beginning of the fourth seminar to the end of the fifth seminar, we will have to encourage people to repent and to have faith. We will do it in the discussions, we will do it in personal contacts after the discussion group this week, we will do it when we prepare them to be prayed with next week, we will do it as we pray with them, we will do it after we pray with them. Our main service during all this time is to encourage people. Only very rarely should we have to be hard with people. Occasionally we need to tell them in straight language that they have to repent and that things will go badly for them if they do not. We have to be prepared to do this when it is appropriate. More normally, however, people will be having problems with fear and doubt. Paul said to "encourage the fainthearted" (I Th 5:13), and that is what we have to do.

The people need to be assured of God's love, and they need to be as assured that God is faithful to his promises. They need personal assurance. They need to know that the problems they are experiencing are normal problems. They need to know that God's promises actually apply to them personally. They need to know that they can give up certain forms of wrongdoing and that the absence of that wrongdoing will not make them unhappy for the rest of their lives. They need to feel our love and concern. They need to have the facts placed before them. In short, they need to be encouraged to take their first steps.

When we are giving people advice about confession, it would be good to recommend a priest who is familiar with the dynamics of the seminars and who would pray with them.

(The discussion) When the discussion leader shares how he turned to the Lord and how he experienced being baptized in the Spirit, he should not give a repeat of what he said in the discussion in the first seminar or in the third seminar. Rather, he should center on what he had to do to repent and how he came to have faith and what the experience of being baptized in the Spirit was like. His testimony should be restricted to the topic of the presentation.

(Additional help) This is the week to find people to help in the fifth seminar. Usually it is good for each discussion leader to have someone to help him pray with the people in his discussion group.

# SEMINAR 4

# Expanded Outline
## of the Presentation

### Introduction

God loves us (Seminar #1); God freed us from darkness and the power of Satan through Jesus Christ (Seminar #2); God wants to give us a new life through the Holy Spirit (Seminar #3). God is offering us a relationship in which we can have new life. He will give us the gift of new life in the Spirit; he will change and heal us, make us new; he will join us to a Christian community or to other brothers and sisters who will help us grow in this new life. We have to turn to him to allow him to do what he is offering to do.

I. In order to receive the new life God is offering us, we must turn away from those things which block our relationship with God and accept Jesus as our Lord.

   A. We need a change of direction, a reorientation of our lives:

   1. away from those things which block our relationship with God and give Satan a hold on us;

   2. towards God and obedience
      - only when we follow him can he lead us to a new life
      - God does not want the obedience of slaves, who obey out of fear of punishment, or the obedience of employees, who obey because they are rewarded; he wants the obedience of sons who obey out of love and respect for their father.

   — We must accept Jesus as our Lord.

  3. The word "repentance" refers to this change of direction.

**B.** Repentance involves:

  1. Honesty

   — the admission that there are things in our lives that are wrong and need changing;

  2. Humility

   — the willingness to change; the awareness that we need God's help;

  3. Renunciation

   — turning away from wrongdoing; deciding not to do it again;

  4. Asking forgiveness for what we have done wrong.

**C.** We must specifically turn away from non-Christian religions, spiritualism, witchcraft, occultism, sexual intercourse outside of marriage, adultery, homosexual acts, murder, robbery, shoplifting, cheating (business deals, on exams), lying, slander, drunkenness (not drinking), getting "stoned" on drugs.

**D.** Those who have committed serious sins need sacramental confession in order to complete their process of reconciliation. Sacramental confession can also be very helpful for those who have not committed serious sins, but who are turning to the Lord in a new way.

**II.** In order to receive the new life God is offering to us, we must ask him for it in faith, expecting to receive it because he wants us to have it and he promised he would give it to us.

 **A.** Faith means relying on what God has said (Matt. 14:22-33).

  1. We know that everything God says is true, be-

cause he knows everything and does not lie:
   — our Christian lives are based on *facts;* we put
      *faith* in the facts, *our feelings follow*
   — we deal with feelings of doubt by looking at
      the facts.
2. When we see the fact that God promised us
   something, we can expect that it will happen
   to us
   — we need more than doctrinal belief alone, we
      need to claim the promises of God.

B.  We can expect God to baptize us in the Spirit:
    1. Because he told us that he wants it for us
       (Luke 11:9-13), because he loves us and
       wants us to be united with him;
    2. We can have it because of what Jesus did for
       us, not because we can earn it or deserve it.

C.  If a Catholic has not been confirmed, he should
    be in order for his initiation as a Catholic to be
    complete. Prayer for release of the Spirit does
    not take the place of the sacrament of confir-
    mation.

III. Next week you will be able to pray with others to
     be baptized in the Spirit, and when you do, you will
     be.

A.  Next week there will be an opportunity to be
    prayed with to be baptized in the Spirit. We
    can ask for the full life of God's Spirit by:
    1. Calling upon the Father in prayer, claiming
       Christ's promise to give us the Holy Spirit
       (Luke 11:13);
    2. At the same time, members of the commu-
       nity/prayer group will pray for you with the
       laying on of hands to ask the Father to fully
       release the Spirit in you.

**B.** What we can expect to have happen:

1. What happened at the first Pentecost: "And they were all filled with the Holy Spirit and began to speak in tongues as the Spirit gave them utterance" (Acts 2:4)
   - something did happen — they were filled with the Holy Spirit
   - *all* were filled, not just some
   - they themselves did something; they began to speak in other tongues as the Spirit gave them utterance.

2. We can expect God to touch us personally with the power of his Spirit.

3. Initial experience varies from individual to individual; some effects are: experiencing the presence of God in a new way, peace and joy, tongues, prophecy.

**C.** Obstacles to receiving God's gifts include:
   - a feeling of unworthiness
   - the fear of making a fool of oneself
   - the fear of having our personalities taken over
   - doubt, temptation by Satan to not believe or to reject God's gifts
   - pride — the feeling that we don't need God's gifts
   - the fear of what others think.

**IV.** Mary has been traditionally seen as the model for Christians receiving the action of the Holy Spirit into their lives. (Luke 1:26-38)

**A.** Mary was the representative of the human race, who, as the mother of the savior, made it possible for God to become man. It was by the overshadowing of her by the Holy Spirit that Jesus was born.

B. Mary accepted her call from God in obedience and in faith in the word that had been spoken to her, (Cf. Luke 1:45, "Blessed is she who believed that there would be a fulfillment of what was spoken to her from the Lord.")

After the discussion: explain the format of Seminar #5. Show them the copy of the commitment to Christ in *Finding New Life in the Spirit*.


# COMMENTS ON THE PRESENTATION

The scriptures mention three things which a person has to do to become a Christian: believe (Mark 16:16), repent (Acts 2:38), and be baptized (Mark 16:16, Acts 2:38). They also say that a person has to do these same things in order to receive the gift of the Spirit and experience spiritual gifts (Mark 16:16, Acts 2:38). These scriptural passages were originally intended to apply to a non-Christian making an initial conversion, but they can also apply to a Christian who is seeking to renew his commitment to the Lord and looking for a deeper experience of the power of the Spirit in his life. For someone who is first becoming a Christian, repentance means a total reorientation of life, faith must include an acceptance of basic Christian truths, and baptism means a sacramental baptism. For someone who is already a Christian, the most important element is a faith that they can receive the full working of the Spirit, although it is essential for them to put away any serious wrongdoing. Baptism, in this case, means something more like "renewal of baptism."

Repentance, faith, baptism and the gift of the Spirit are all parts of the covenant which God has made with us. A covenant has two parts: the promise of what the other person will do, and the conditions that we have to fulfill. God's promise to us is the gift of the Holy Spirit; our part is repentance, faith, and receiving the sacrament. Repentance, faith, and submitting to being baptized are our turning to the Lord; in response, God gives us the Holy Spirit. Something like this happens when we renew our baptism by being baptized in the Holy Spirit. Asking to be baptized in the Spirit is an expression of our repentance and faith, and of our desire to be truly renewed and begin a deeper Christian life. The Lord wants this even more than we do, so we can ask with expectant faith that he will release in us the power of the Holy Spirit that will renew us. It is the Lord who baptizes us in the Spirit.

(I) In the first section of the talk we are concerned with something that is very simple, and in a way, primitive. We must make clear to people that they must put away anything which blocks their relationship to God. We are primarily concerned with any major things that they are doing wrong, things which are incompatible with the Christian life. We are not so much concerned with things which, while they could block deeper growth in Christian life, are not serious enough to block a person from being baptized in the Spirit.

There are two kinds of repentance for a Christian: basic repentance and advanced repentance. Basic repentance is concerned with "big sins", wrongdoing that is incompatible with Christianity. Paul gives a list of different types of such wrongdoing in I Cor 5:11 and 6:9-10. There is another list in Rev 21:9. Similar lists are scattered throughout the scriptures. This is wrongdoing which breaks the commandments of God, which no one who calls Jesus his Lord can still engage in. Advanced repentance, on the other hand, is concerned with faults that block our Christian progress, faults such as watching television too much, not praying enough, not giving enough of our money to the poor.

There are two reasons for centering on basic repentance in this talk. The first is simply that many people need basic repentance and not advanced repentance. If we center on advanced repentance, we often pass over serious sins. More "good Christians" come to the Life in the Spirit Seminars with serious wrongdoing in their lives than most team members believe.

The second reason for centering on basic repentance is that people often find ideas like "let Christ tell us everything we do", of "giving up everything", or "dying to ourselves" a burden that they are not ready to bear. A "total dedication" talk on repentance often confuses and worries people. They begin to fear that Christ will ask them to give up all their money, or dictate whom they must marry. Now, Christ may well ask a person for all of his money or tell him whom he should marry, but he usually prepares him for it before he asks him. At this point, it is important to get people into the right kind of relationship with the Holy Spirit so that they can be given a desire to do everything Christ wants. Once they start to fall in love with Jesus, they are ready for advanced repentance.

(I.A) "Repentance" and "obedience" are closely related. The Lord wants us to obey him. If we are not obeying him, if we are doing something that he does not want us to do, we have to change. The scriptures use the word "repentance" to describe that change. Repentance is not feeling bad about what we have done (although that may be a part of it), it is an actual change of direction, a turning towards obedience.

(I.B.3,4) The word "wrongdoing" is used in the talk rather than the word "sin". "Sin" can imply many things. It can imply a whole condition of being out of God's plan. It often carries connotations of blame and feelings of guilt. "Wrongdoing" makes a clear, simple point: people have to stop doing things that are wrong and begin to do the things that are right.

**(I.C)** We want to mention common types of serious wrongdoing. Different groups of people may need to have different types of wrongdoing mentioned.

When we talk about robbery, cheating, lying, etc., we are talking about serious robbery, cheating, lying, etc. We are not talking about small offenses. Small offenses should also be done away with, but our concern here is to center on serious wrongdoing.

When we speak against drunkenness, we do not want to convey the impression that we think drinking is wrong in itself. Nor do we want to tell people that smoking is incompatible with Christianity. We also want to avoid taking a "hard line" on drugs. We do not want to say that taking drugs in itself is wrong, but we want to say that allowing any sort of damaging effects to ourselves—getting out of control, harming our mind, impairing our ability to function—is wrong. (In effect, this is to say that people should not take drugs.) Our objective is to avoid all puritanism. People may decide that it is better not to smoke or drink or take drugs. That is their decision as the Spirit leads them. We do not want to say that something is incompatible with Christianity when the Lord did not say it was incompatible.

**(II)** The second section should be a simple instruction on faith. For many people this will be the most important section of the talk. This may be the first time that they have been instructed in the importance of an active, expectant faith. For many this may also be the first time they are taught to put faith first, and not feelings.

Throughout the talk and the seminars, we want people to focus on Christ and his promises, not on having faith. If people start concentrating on their own faith, they will have a hard time having faith. It is when they have their eyes on the Lord, on his power and his promises that faith will grow in them. Above all, we should not tell them that they *must* have faith (or even worse, that they cannot doubt) in order to be baptized in the Spirit. We should encourage people to have faith, not demand it of them. Besides, God will often work even in people who do not have much faith.

(II.C) The main purpose of this statement is to make clear once again the relationship of the sacraments of initiation to prayer for being baptized in the Spirit. Presumably, all who come will have been baptized and confirmed.

(III) The final section prepares people for the fifth seminar. It gives them a concrete idea of the way they will be helped to be baptized in the Spirit. We should talk about what will happen with maximum faith, encouraging them to expect the Spirit to work in them powerfully. We should not speak to them about it cautiously, timidly, or hesitantly. The Lord will meet their faith.

# SEMINAR 5

# Praying For Baptism In The Holy Spirit

---

## GOAL

To help people make an authentic commitment to Christ, to help them to be baptized in the Spirit and speak in tongues.

---

"And when Paul had laid his hands upon them, the Holy Spirit came on them; and they spoke with tongues and prophesied."
(Acts 19:7)

The fifth week is the turning point of the seminars, the moment at which many of the people in the seminar begin a new life with Christ. For ourselves, it can be a real time of renewal and rededication, one of the times when we can feel most assured that we are performing a genuine service for the Lord.

However, we should not approach the fifth week as if it were to be the culmination of a person's Christian life. Our attitude should not be, "This is it, we've reached the summit", but "Now let's get started". We want to convey in both what we say and do that it is the life in the Spirit, the life of following Christ, that is important, not the experience of being baptized in the Spirit.

# The Fifth Team Meeting

1. Review last week's seminar
   - discuss any problems that appeared and what to do about them
   - go over the list of people and consider what should be done for them
2. Preview the fifth seminar
   - understand the goal to be achieved (not just a spiritual experience, but a new relationship with Christ)
   - review the whole seminar paying attention to seating, tone, etc.
3. Discuss how to pray with people
   - the prayer of exorcism
   - how to help people relax, focus on the Lord
   - how to help them yield to tongues and other spiritual gifts
   - looking to the Lord for guidance
4. Pray for the seminar and the people in it

# The Fifth Seminar

A. A Brief Explanation Of The Meeting By The Team Leader

   —introduce any new people who have come to help

   1. Explain the prayer session
      - the commitment to Christ
      - the prayer of exorcism
      - the laying on of hands (asking in faith)
   2. Explain how to yield to tongues

140

3. Call to mind right attitudes
4. Ask them not to leave until the whole group is done praying so that we can all end at the same time.

B. **The Prayer Session**

1. Opening song and prayer
2. The team leader asks the questions and leads the people in the prayer of commitment (each person responds to the question individually, unless the group is too large; the whole group recites the prayer after him).
3. All pray together to ask the Lord's blessing and begin to praise him.
4. Those who are praying over people command any evil spirits to depart, lay hands on each person, and ask the Lord to baptize them in his Spirit. They counsel them if necessary.
5. When everyone is done the team leader draws the whole group together. He teaches them about singing in tongues, leading them in spontaneous praise and singing in the Spirit.

C. **Closing Exhortation**

1. Different people have different experiences.
2. Be aware that Satan can tempt one to doubt.
3. You can't expect all your problems to go away at once, although many of them will.
4. Be faithful in daily prayer, and make a good part of it prayer of praise and thanksgiving. Pray in tongues every day. If you are involved in a community or prayer group, attend the meetings faithfully.

D. **Concluding Song And Greeting**

E. **(Optional) Celebration of the Eucharist**

# COMMENTS ON THE DYNAMICS

Above all — turn to the Lord and put faith in him. The more the team is centered on the Lord and the more the team has faith, the easier it will be for the people. Faith "catches." In an atmosphere of worship and faith, it is much easier to have faith.

There should also be an atmosphere of peace. We do not want to encourage emotional excitement. Rather, we want to encourage relaxed joy. A quiet room or place should be chosen where there is the least noise and distractions. Those conducting the prayers should be warm and friendly and relaxed and should themselves convey a mood of peace and calmness to those who are seeking to be baptized in the Spirit.

The team should be especially open to spiritual gifts during this time. The prayer room should be "charismatic." The Lord will work through the team with prophecy and words of wisdom, with discernment and faith, even with healing. If we obey the promptings of the Spirit, we will see God work in many ways that we might not have expected.

(Yielding to tongues) People should come to see tongues as another means of growing closer to Christ. It is a gift we can all use right from the start of our new entrance into the life of God's Spirit. A person should claim this gift in confidence when he is prayed with to be baptized in the Spirit. No one needs to wait for this gift or shy away from it because of unworthiness. It is a gift God gives freely, simply because we ask for it. No one has to "psych himself up" or feel emotionally ready to receive the gift.

Three conditions dispose us to receive the gift of tongues. First, we should desire this gift; we should hunger and thirst for the gifts of God. Paul said, "Make love your aim and earnestly desire the spiritual gifts" (1 Cor. 14:1). This includes tongues. Second, we should ask in faith for the gift. Faith means looking to Christ expectantly for him to give it to us. Third, we must cooperate with God by speaking out in faith and expecting God to give us the utterance. What we need is active faith, not passive faith.

There are some people who come seeking to be baptized in the Spirit who say that they do not want to have the gift of tongues. This is a wrong attitude. The person is placing limits on God's working, he is not being open to the Lord. Everyone should want to have tongues.

Tongues may not be of first importance in itself, but it has great consequences in a person's spiritual life. It can revolutionize a person's prayer life. A person who prays in tongues can normally pray much more easily, and his prayer will be more likely to be filled with praise and worship. But even more significantly, tongues usually turns out to be the gateway to the charismatic dimension. It builds a person's faith in a very concrete way. It gives him a clear experience of what it means to have the Holy Spirit work through him – an experience of him being fully active and yet the Holy Spirit forming something new through him. Yielding to tongues is an important first step, and it is worth putting effort into encouraging a person to yield to tongues, even to run the risk of being labeled "imbalanced".

At the same time, we should make it clear that speaking in tongues is neither a necessary sign, nor by itself a certain sign, that a person has been baptized in the Spirit. We should encourage people to be open to this gift, as a valuable way of praying, especially in praising God, but we should not put so much stress on it that their attention will be on tongues, and not on the Lord and his gift of the Holy Spirit.

(B.2) The commitment to Christ can be understood as a renewal of our baptismal vows. A definite clear verbal commitment is a help to a person's decision to be a follower of Christ (Rom 10:9).

(B.3). Some groups have found it helpful to begin by leading everyone in collective prayer that the Lord will release his Holy Spirit and give the gift of tongues. Other groups prefer to have two or three team members or other mature Christians pray over each person individually. Both approaches are effective. The Lord will baptize people in his Spirit and give them the gift of tongues whether the prayer is primarily collective or primarily individual.

If the team decides to lead a group prayer that the Lord act, there should be time for brief individual prayer over each new person afterward. This should include a prayer of thanksgiving to the Lord and encouragement to the person who has been baptized in the Spirit. Some people may need help in yielding to tongues. If the prayer is primarily collective, it is especially important to establish an atmosphere of relaxed, free, and spontaneous praise. To assist in this, the team members may invite some other mature members of the prayer group or community to pray with the group during the fifth session.

If the prayer is primarily individual, those in the room should pray in low voices. The sound of prayer provides privacy for those being prayed with to be baptized in the Spirit. Everyone in the room should be praying throughout the prayer session.

(B.4 - exorcism). Before group prayer, the leader should say a short prayer of exorcism for everyone. Before individual prayer, the team member should say the prayer of exorcism simply and undramatically, in a quiet voice, so that only those who are praying with a particular person will hear it.

The team member should simply command whatever evil spirits are there to depart. The Lord will ordinarily provide some kind of discernment if the team member has faith for it (often it takes time to grow in that faith). If the team member has some discernment, he should simply command that spirit to depart.

"Exorcism" is simply a traditional word for either casting out evil spirits or telling evil spirits to leave a person or a place free. In explaining the prayer of exorcism we should say that we are simply going to pray the same kind of prayer that is part of every Catholic celebration of the sacrament of baptism. We are not talking about the kind of exorcism that is called for when there is reason to judge that an individual is actually possessed or obsessed. Some prefer to use the term "praying for deliverance from evil spirits." This term is a good one, but it can be misleading. We do not ask God to free the person from evil spirits. We take the authority God has given us (Mk 16:17) and command the evil spirit to go.

(B.4 - praying with people). When praying with people individually to be baptized in the Spirit, it is good to pray in teams of twos. Having a number of teams allows several people to be prayed with at the same time (avoiding having everyone waiting for a long time while others are being prayed with). Praying in twos provides communal support which is helpful. The discussion leaders should pray with those in their groups.

When praying with people to be baptized in the Spirit, we should apply the right amount of encouragement and understanding for each person. Some people will yield to the Spirit beautifully without any encouragement at all. Some will need just a little push. Some will need patient encouragement. Some should not be pushed at all. We have to let the Spirit lead us and give us wisdom in how to help people.

Often people can be helped to yield to tongues rather easily. Many, perhaps most, will not understand or follow the instructions given in the opening remarks. After praying with a person to be baptized in the Spirit, the team member should lean over or kneel down and ask the person if he would like to pray in tongues. When he says yes, he should encourage him to speak out, making sounds that are not English. He can say many of the same things that are in the opening remarks (A2). He should then pray with him again.

When the person begins to speak in tongues, he should encourage him. Many will still be afraid that it is "just them". The team member can often supply the faith that will allow them to yield to the Spirit.

(B.5) To teach people how to sing in tongues, the team leader should simply explain that it is like speaking in tongues, except that the Holy Spirit also forms the melody. He encourages them to turn to Christ and to begin to sing, yielding to the Spirit and allowing the Spirit to form the melody. The whole group should sing in tongues easily.

(E.) A Eucharistic celebration at this point can be very appropriate. Just as the sacraments of initiation in the early church concluded with the catechumens joining the other Christians for a Eucharistic celebration, it is fitting that the renewal of initiation conclude with a Eucharistic celebration. There are, however, often practical reasons for not having a Eucharist at the same time as praying over people. Very often, there is not adequate time in an evening to do both well. Enough time should be taken to pray with people well, giving them the attention they need and allowing them enough time to respond to the Lord. Above all, the prayer session should not be ritualized, but people should be helped individually and prayed with as long as is helpful. It might be possible to lengthen the seminars by a week and conclude the whole course by a Eucharistic celebration. It might also be possible to have a Eucharistic celebration at another time during the week.

# SEMINAR 5

# Expanded Outline
## of the Presentation

A. **Introductory Explanation**

  1. We are here to claim Christ's promise of the Holy Spirit (Lk 11:13)

Explain what will happen in the prayer session (mention the commitment ceremony, the prayer of exorcism, how people will pray over them). Explain that the prayer session for the release of the Holy Spirit is modelled on the ceremony for the initiation of a Christian.

The Lord is the baptizer in the Holy Spirit. We will lay hands on you and pray with you. You ask him to give what he promised and expect it.

Different things will happen to different people. Don't seek a particular kind of experience. Just turn to the Lord and receive a new life in the Holy Spirit from him.

  2. How to yield to tongues

Tongues comes when a person is baptized in the Holy Spirit.

Everyone should want the gift of tongues, it is a gift of God.

We would never say to the Lord, "I want what you have for me, except _____."

Do not expect the Holy Spirit to force you to speak in tongues, you have have to yield to it. The Holy Spirit does not "take us over". He leaves us our freedom.

— "they spoke in other tongues as the Spirit gave

utterance" (Acts 2:4) — we speak, the Spirit forms the speech. If the Spirit would inspire us to write a letter, we would have to sit down and write; so when the Spirit inspires us to speak in tongues, we have to speak.

— after you ask to be baptized in the Holy Spirit and ask for the gift of tongues, then yield to it. Begin by speaking out, if necessary beginning by just making meaningless sounds. The Holy Spirit will form them.

— the steering wheel of a car can be turned more easily when the car is in motion, so the Holy Spirit can form the gift of tongues in us more readily when we are speaking.

— don't pray in English or in any language you know.

Don't be afraid that it is just you, and not the Spirit.

Don't be analyzing the sounds. Don't worry if it seems like babble or baby talk.

Make the sounds an act of worship to God. Focus on him, not on the sounds.

Some of you may also be given words of prophecy in English, a message or an inspired prayer. Yield to it and speak out.

3. Some important right attitudes

Relax. The more relaxed we are, the easier it is to receive the Lord's gifts. It is much harder to put something in a clenched fist than in an open relaxed hand.

Don't be afraid of sounding foolish.

The Lord loves you and wants you to experience his love in a new way.

4. Please do not leave after you are prayed with, but wait so that we can all end together.

While you are waiting, pray for your brothers and

sisters and praise the Lord.

We want an atmosphere of prayer to pervade the room until we are finished.

B. **The prayer session**

1. Opening song and prayer

2. The commitment to Christ

Do you renounce Satan and all wrongdoing?

Do you believe that Jesus is the Son of God, that he died to free us from our sins, and that he rose to bring us new life?

Will you follow Jesus as your Lord?

Lord Jesus Christ, I want to belong to you from now on. I want to be free from the dominion of darkness and the rule of Satan, and I want to enter into your kingdom and be part of your people. I will turn away from all wrongdoing, and I will avoid everything that leads me to wrongdoing. I ask you to forgive all the sins that I have committed. I offer my life to you, and I promise to obey you as my Lord. I ask you to baptize me in the Holy Spirit.

C. Closing exhortation

1. Different people have different experiences.

Feeling is not the important thing. Look for the new ways God is at work in you and respond to it: a new desire for prayer, for scripture, etc.

If you did not speak in tongues tonight, don't worry about it! Expect it to come soon. Don't make the mistake of identifying "being baptized in the Spirit" with "getting the gift of tongues." In your prayer during this coming week, give plenty of time to praise and thanksgiving, doing this aloud, if you can do so without disturbing anyone, and you may well discover that you can praise the Lord in tongues. But whether in tongues or with your own words is not so important as that you praise and thank him for his gift of the Spirit. If you were not sure, just keep doing what you were doing and ask the Lord to form it into the gift of tongues if it isn't.

2. Be aware that Satan can tempt one to doubt.

Satan is seeking to rob everyone of God's gift. For him the next best thing to keeping you from getting it is to keep you from using it. If he can convince you that the key in your hand is not the key to the door, he can keep you from using it to open the door.

Don't let feelings of doubt bother you. Remember the fact that God promised it and you asked for it.

3. You can't expect all your problems to go away at once, though many will.

The Holy Spirit will make a big change in you, and you will see it. But not everything will be changed. Some things will take a while to get worked out. But now you have a new power to use in working them out.

4. Be faithful to a regular time of daily prayer and to regular participation in the meetings of your local community or prayer group. Pray in tongues every day. Be sure that a good portion of your prayer time is spent in praise and thanksgiving, in your own words.

"He who is faithful with a little will be set over much" (Mt 25:21).

What happened tonight is just a beginning.

5. Go easy in your sharing of this with others.

It is possible to scare people off, to give them more

than they are ready for.

The first thing to do is to love them more than you did before and serve them. The change in you will be a witness to Christ.

Go easiest with those who are closest to you — especially your family.

We'll be talking about how to share what we've found in the seminar next week. We'll also be talking about how to grow in it. You need instruction more now that you have been baptized in the Holy Spirit than you did before.

# COMMENTS ON THE PRESENTATION

Little more is needed than what is written on the expanded outline. The remarks should be simple and clear. They are intended to focus attitudes and encourage faith. The less talking and the more prayer the better.

# SEMINAR 6

# Growth

---

## GOAL

**To help them to make a commitment to take the steps they need to take to ensure that they will grow in the life of the Spirit.**

---

"I am the vine, you are the branches. He who abides in me and I in him, he it is that bears much fruit, for apart from me you can do nothing."

(Jn 15:5)

The sixth week is a week for solid growth. The people in the seminar have begun something new. Now they must be taught practical ways to make what they have begun into something solid, something that will last. Like the fourth week, the sixth week is practical and instructional, teaching people how to take definite steps.

# The Sixth Team Meeting

1.   Review last week's seminar
     - discuss any problems that appeared and what to do about them
     - go over the list of people and consider what should be done for them
2.   Preview the sixth seminar
     - understand the goal to be achieved
     - go over the discussion and the discussion question, being clear on what the discussion should accomplish
3.   Discuss how to help people who have had problems since last week
     - those to whom nothing seemed to happen
     - those who haven't prayed in tongues (to their own satisfaction)
     - those who have already run into some problem or difficulty
4.   Discuss how to help in the new phase (moving from the Life in the Spirit Seminars to an ongoing life in the Spirit)
     - encouraging them to make the commitments they need to make
     - helping them make connection with the community or prayer group
5.   Pray for the seminar and the people in it

# The Sixth Seminar

A. **The Talk**

1. In order to grow in the life of the Spirit, we have to make use of the basic means to growth, especially personal prayer and being part of a community.
2. We should spend time with the Lord in prayer every day.
3. We should be part of a Christian community/prayer group.
4. We should peacefully share what we have found with others.

B. **The Discussion Group**

Discussion starter: Share what has happened to you since last week. After discussing what has happened to people since last week and any problems brought to light in the sharing, the leader should encourage a discussion on prayer and community, if such a discussion does not come out of the sharing. He should share his own personal experience of both.

C. **Personal Contact**

After the discussions, the team members should use the time to talk with anyone who seems to have a problem he needs help with, or to make an appointment to get together with him.

## COMMENTS ON THE DYNAMICS

The week after the fifth seminar is usually very different for different people in the seminar. People will run the whole range of reactions and emotions. The most common reactions are: complete euphoria (the person has had an emotional and spiritual experience which has left him feeling freer and happier than he has ever felt before); a feeling of "I hope it lasts" (this person is already experiencing some doubts and fears that he may "lose it" if he isn't careful); disappointment (the person was let down because the experience was not what he had anticipated, or because he did not pray in tongues); and a reaction which has embraced all of these feelings in the short space of a week (perhaps the most common category).

Each one of these reactions must be dealt with gently and lovingly. Each person should see that the team member understands what he is going through and that he is more than willing to talk or pray about it with him. The team member must not squash the euphoria, nor demand from anyone more than he can give, nor brush off as unimportant or ridiculous anyone's disappointments or doubts. The sixth seminar should be a time when people begin to move away from approaching the life of the Spirit by their feelings and begin to approach it in faith. Those who are disappointed must be encouraged to have faith. They should probably be prayed with again for tongues or just encouraged to keep on praying those sounds that they are dissatisfied with. We should help others center their euphoria on serving the Lord. All should be encouraged to make the Word of the Lord their foundation.

(The discussion) There are a number of reasons for sharing how the past week has been:

— it gives people a chance to see that they are not alone, whether their week was good, bad, indifferent, or all three. As people see that others had a week similar to theirs, there is often a visible relief on some of the faces;

— through the sharing they can help one another: "Yes, I

had that feeling too, this is what I did about it";

— it lets the team know where people are at and gives leads on the kind of help that people need;

— it gives the disappointed a chance to be accepted, even though they are afraid that they have not "measured up".

The team should use the discussion as a time to encourage people to go on with further growth (to be led by the Spirit or to pray more) as well as to help them with their problems.

# SEMINAR 6

# Expanded Outline
# of the Presentation

I.  In order to grow in the life of the Spirit, we have to make use of the basic means of growth

A.  Being baptized in the Spirit is only a beginning; now we need to grow in the life of the Spirit.

B.  In order to grow, each of us needs certain practices in our lives: prayer, study, service, and community.
    — explain the wheel diagram.
    1. The power that comes from the Holy Spirit makes us grow.
    2. But we need to keep in contact with Christ in order for the Holy Spirit to keep strengthening us.
    3. Prayer, study, service and community are means to growth, ways of staying in contact with Christ.

C.  The Christian life is not something we live on our own, but with the rest of the Christian people.
    — among other things, this especially means regular participation in the liturgy of the church.

II. We should spend time with the Lord in prayer every day

A.  Personal relationships (friendships) don't grow without two people spending time together, so we have to spend time with the Lord to grow in our relationship with him.

B.  We can expect the Lord to speak to us and reveal himself to us if we give him a chance.

C.  Set aside time every day for prayer and scripture reading.
  — decide on a particular time
  — find a place
  — the daily Office can be helpful.

Include personal testimony to the value of a daily period for prayer. Mention study briefly.

III. We should be part of a Christian community/prayer group

A.  We have to get together regularly with a group of Christians with whom we can grow in what we've found.

B.  Community is not an optional extra, it is essential to the life of the Spirit.
  1. God's plan is for us to come to him with others, in a body.
  2. The Holy Spirit works through others to build us up — this is what spiritual gifts are.
  3. The result of Pentecost was to create a community of Christians (Acts 2:41-47).

C.  Church life as it exists in most parishes is not enough. To grow in the life of the Spirit we need to get together with Christians who have experienced the same thing we have.
  — The Lord does not want us to leave the Church, but to become more active, better members of it.

D.  Explain how to make contact with the community or prayer group (briefly here).

Include personal testimony to the value of community.

IV. We should share with others what we have found

A.  One main form of service is to share with others what we have found ourselves.

B.  With our friends and family we should begin by

showing them the kind of love that they can experience as love, by showing them the fruit of our changed lives.

C.   We should then share with them about the Lord as they seem open, not being too pushy or frightening them unnecessarily but not being unwilling to talk with them about the Lord.

# COMMENTS ON THE PRESENTATION

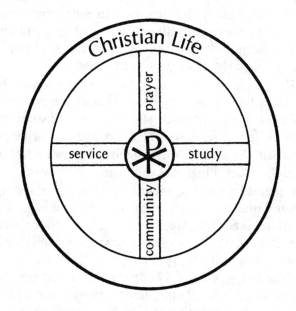

(1) The wheel diagram: The Christian life can be pictured as a wheel. The *rim* of the wheel represents the Christian's daily life. The *hub* of a wheel is the source of

power and direction for the whole wheel. It holds the wheel together. The hub of the Christian life is Christ himself (on the throne, the center). In order to transmit the power and direction from the hub to the rim, *spokes* are needed. Some spokes in the Christian life are prayer, study, service and community. These are means to put our whole life in contact with Christ, so that he can transform it with his power and directions.

The purpose of the wheel diagram is to put into people's lives practices by which they can grow as Christians. It does not seek to explain the mediation of Christ's presence to individuals. Therefore, it focuses upon basic means of growth, not the presence of Christ in groups of committed Christians, the body of Christ, or the sacraments. In the course of the presentation we want to encourage people to participate in the regular liturgical life of the church, but this talk is simply designed to recommend certain practical means by which they can grow as Christians.

(II) The section on prayer should be an encouragement to spending time in prayer. It can be a simple presentation, but should have personal sharing. The speaker should describe different ways that he prays and that other people pray so that the people in the seminar can get a feel of the range of different things that can happen in prayer.

It would be good to mention briefly that the scripture is read and understood within the church, as it is given to us in Christian Tradition. We should not just rely on the way we can understand it with the personal light the Holy Spirit gives each of us individually.

There is a very helpful book on prayer that the speaker can recommend here—Ralph Martin's *Hungry for God: Practical Help in Personal Prayer*. The book explains in greater depth the role of prayer in a relationship with God. Its practical advice is excellent for people who are trying to build or maintain a regular prayer life.

160

(III)   The purpose of the section on community is to begin the process of winning people to commit themselves to other Christians and to an ongoing effort to grow with them and to serve with them in the Christian life. In this section we mainly stress the fact that community is part of God's plan. In the next seminar, the practical need for help from others is stressed.

Personal testimony can be used effectively in this section. If the speaker can share how community has been of personal value, the people in the seminar will be more open to it.

(III.C)   Most Christian parishes and congregations do not constitute the kind of community in which people share their lives with one another and help one another to grow in the life of the Spirit. Prayer groups and communities of the charismatic renewal are meeting a need which a great many are feeling today.

We want to encourage people to be active church members and good parishioners. This is not necessarily an encouragement for them to get involved in many church activities. Many will, in fact, need to cut down on the activities in their lives. We should encourage them to seek the right kind of involvement so that they are good church members and so that they are growing in the Lord and serving the Lord better. Whether they should take on more church activities is a matter for individual discernment.

Many who experience a release of the Spirit, especially if they have not been active enough church members before, will experience a disappointment in the Sunday liturgy or even weekday liturgy, unless they are carefully oriented toward them. The liturgy is meant to be an important part of our spiritual life, yet we should not speak about it in a way that ignores present difficulties connected with it. We should simply indicate its importance and express a confidence that as the church is renewed, the parish and the lit-

161

urgy can become all that they are meant to be. We are not to become critical, but we should participate as servants, looking for the ways that the new life in us can be shared with others.

(IV)   In the fourth section of the talk we want to do two things:   1) we want to encourage the people in the seminars to tell others about Christ and about the new life they have found (explicit, verbal witness/evangelism); 2) we want to avoid having them come on too strong or too hard or too fast. Evangelism with those who are close to us has to proceed carefully. But it should proceed and not be avoided.

(IV.A)   If we love others, we will want to share with them the good things we have found. It will be a natural overflow of our new life.

(IV.B) Those who are close to us can be threatened easily. If they see a sudden change in us or if they feel that we are trying to convert them or otherwise change them, they can become very fearful and closed. We have to make our first concern to make them know that we love them more, not to make our first concern to preach the gospel to them. Once they experience something new in us they like, they will be more open to listen.

Different people react different ways to what we want to share with them about our new life in the Spirit. When our relationship with someone is bad or problematic in some way, it is usually good to go slow. We can be freer when we have a close, warm, trusting friendship with someone.

(IV.C) On the other hand, we should not be unwilling to speak to people about what we have discovered. They will rarely find the new life we have found if they are not told something about it.

## HELPFUL MATERIALS
During the sixth seminar, the team members might

help new people choose reading material which will help them grow in the Christian life. *New Covenant* magazine provides regular monthly teaching articles to foster spiritual growth. (A *New Covenant* subscription blank can be found in the back of the booklet *Finding New Life in the Spirit*.)

Several books in the *Living as a Christian* series are especially useful to help people grow in the Christian life. These include *Growing in Faith* and *Knowing God's Will*, both by Steve Clark; *God First, Decision to Love,* and *Sons and Daughters of God*, all by Ken Wilson; and *Growing Closer to God* by Tom Gryn. The team members might also recommend such books as *Reading Scripture as the Word of God* by George Martin and *The Purpose of Temptation* by Bob Mumford. (See the discussion of reading material on pp. 43-44.)

# SEMINAR 7

# Transformation In Christ

---

## GOAL

To help people avoid discouragement over problems they experience, and to help them become part of a charismatic community or prayer group.

---

"Not that I am already perfect; but I press on to make it my own, because Christ Jesus has made me his own."                    (Phil 3:12)

The final seminar is a combination of two things: more instruction on how to grow in the Christian life and direction on how to make the kind of connection that is necessary in order to go on growing in the life of the Spirit. The last seminar can be a time of great warmth and love. It can also be a time of working through difficulties. It should be a time of commitment to go on and encouragement to go on.

# The Seventh Team Meeting

1. Go over last week's seminar — discuss any problems that appeared and what to do about them — go over the list of people and consider what should be done for them
2. Go over the seventh seminar — understand the goal to be achieved — go over the discussion and the discussion question, being clear on what the discussion should accomplish
3. Pray for the seminar and for those in it

# The Seventh Seminar

A. **The Talk** (at least the third part should be given by the team leader)
   1. The Holy Spirit is at work in us to change us and make us holier.
   2. We can expect to experience trials and difficulties as we grow: they can be a means of growth.
   3. In order to grow and overcome difficulties, we need much more than what the Life in the Spirit Seminars have been able to give us.

   Explain fully how to make contact with the community or prayer group.

B. **The Discussion Group**
   Discussion starter: Share about the difficulties or trials you have had since being prayed with and share

165

about the way you handled them. Do you have any questions about how to be a part of the community/prayer group?

C. Concluding Prayer Of Thanksgiving Together


# COMMENTS ON THE DYNAMICS

The last seminar is often a time for the team member to be of special help to people in the seminar. He should approach the last seminar as a chance for service, not as the seminar that comes after the service is ended.

The seminar should end with warmth and love. The team members should greet the people in the seminar with affection.

# Expanded Outline
## of the Presentation

I. The Holy Spirit is at work in us to change us and make us holier.

    A. He is working to draw us into a deeper union with God and one another, to give us a fuller experience of the new life.

    B. He is working to make us realize the need for us to turn away from wrongdoing, to reorder our priorities, to take away all those things that make us less loving.

Include personal sharing on how the Lord is changing us.

II. We can expect to experience trials and difficulties as we grow: they can be a means of growth.

    A. Problems, difficulties and trials are normal and to be expected.

    B. The Lord uses them for our growth.

        1. "God works for the good in everything with those who love him" (Rom. 8:28).

        2. We now have a new power to deal with difficulties.

        3. The Lord will teach us things through overcoming difficulties.

        4. 1 Thess. 5:16-17.

    C. Help is available from the leaders of the community and from members of the community, especially those more mature in the life of the Spirit.

Include personal sharing on how trials and difficulties can be overcome.

III. After the seminars (this part at least should be given by the team leader)

    A. In order to grow, we need much more (the LSS is only a beginning):

        1. We need to learn a great deal more about the Christian life
- it is important to take advantage of the teaching which is available in the community.

        2. We need the strength and support of others, the sharing of experience, advice
- a good way to put out a fire is to pull the logs apart, a good basis for starting a fire is to put them together in the right way.

        3. We need a situation in which we can learn how to serve the Lord.

Include personal testimony to the value of community and its importance for growth in the life of the Spirit.

    B. Explain clearly and at length about the life of the community or prayer group and how to get into it.

# COMMENTS ON THE PRESENTATION

The seventh seminar, like the sixth seminar, is an instructional seminar. Many people, even at this point, still have the feeling that once baptized in the Spirit nothing can go wrong. Such people are in a dangerous position. Satan can use any setback to destroy their faith. The seventh seminar should make clear both that they should expect difficulties and that those difficulties can be a source of great advance.

The seventh seminar should convey a sense of the power and victory of the Lord. Difficulties come, that is true. But the Lord has given us a new power. He is setting us on the path of growth. We do not have to be fearful. We are in his hands, and he will be faithful to us. He wants to make us new men and women.

The seventh seminar should also be the time in which the need for a definite commitment to a definite community or prayer group is presented. The previous week laid the foundation. This week the specifics are presented.

In some ways this is the most important part of the talk. If the people in the seminar do not make the commitment to go on with others, they will probably not be able to go on nearly as well.

The first two parts of the talk should be given with personal examples. The more it is presented in an experiential way, the more effective it will be.

(I) Jesus wants us to enter into a deeper relationship with him every day. He wants us to more and more become as he is—holy and perfect. But how can man make himself holy and perfect as God is holy and perfect? He can't. God himself must bring about our holiness and perfection, and he will if we let him. "God is at work in you, both to will and to work for his good pleasure" (Phil 2:13). "May the God of peace sanctify you wholly; and may your spirit and soul and body be kept sound and blameless at the coming of our Lord Jesus Christ. He who calls you is faithful, and he will do it." (I Thess 5:23-24). Just as Jesus is the one who redeems us and baptizes us in the Holy Spirit, so too is he the one who perfects us. There is no part of our lives which Jesus does not want to perfect in himself. We must, for our part, allow him to show us our imperfections and allow him to change us.

(II) Problems, difficulties and trials must be seen as an opportunity for the grace of God to triumph. The Lord has given us a new power, and that power is at work in every situation.

Problems like doubts, fears, lack of trust, self-pity, temptation; difficulties like distractions and dryness in prayer, mistakes in following the leadings of the Spirit, and trials like persecution or misunderstandings are commonly experienced in these weeks.

(III) The team leader should give the last part of the talk as "fatherly advice". The people in the seminar need to take some concrete steps if they are to go on. They should understand the things they need to do in a clear way, and they should understand that experience indicates that they will not grow without taking these steps.

Unless impossible, the team leader should explain exactly what the people in the seminar have to do to be part of the prayer group or community. He should not just say "you need to be part of some group, and this is how you can be part of this one". Sometimes the advice will simply amount to coming to a weekly prayer meeting each week. Sometimes more will be involved.

HELPFUL MATERIALS

Many books in the *Living as a Christian* series help Christians overcome personal weaknesses and obstacles to growth in the Spirit. Especially recommended are *How to Repair the Wrong You've Done* by Ken Wilson; *Getting Free* and *The Angry Christian* by Bert Ghezzi; and *Living with a Clear Conscience* and *The Self-Image of a Christian* by Mark Kinzer. Other books in the series discuss growth in Christian character and improving personal relationships. *How to Become the Person You Were Meant to Be* by Peter Williamson offers basic teaching about growing in the Spirit. (See the discussion of reading material on pp. 43-44.)

# Concluding Team Meeting

## GOAL
To get an overview of the seminar; to learn from the seminar

1. Go over the list of people and see what happened to
   them
   - did any not find a new relationship with the Lord
     (did any not make a commitment to him, not
     pray in tongues, not want to be part of the
     community/prayer group)?
   - was there something we could have done dif-
     ferently to help them find what they didn't
     find?
   - what did we learn from working with them?
   - can we do something more for them this week or
     in the near future?
2. Go over the seminars
   a. the presentations
      - were they clear?
      - did they get the essential points across?
      - were they too long or too short?
      - did they have a good effect on the people in
        the seminar?
   b. the discussions
      - was there a good spirit of openness and sharing
        in them?
      - did we get the things accomplished in the dis-
        cussions that we needed to get accom-
        plished?
      - what problems did we run into in leading the
        discussions that we didn't know how to
        handle?

c. personal contact
    — did we get it done?
    — were we able to get at the problems?

3. Share what the Lord did with us or taught us while we were working on these seminars

4. Pray for the seminar and the people in it: end with thanksgiving

The team leader should communicate the results of the evaluation to the people in the community who are responsible for the Life in the Spirit Seminars.

# PART THREE

# THE
# GREETERS TEAM

In the fifteenth chapter of Romans, Paul says to the
Christians at Rome:

> "Welcome one another, therefore, as Christ has wel-
> comed you, for the glory of God."    (Rom 15:7)

Paul was actually speaking about the attitude that Christians
should maintain towards one another in their communities,
but the model he holds up is the attitude that Christ takes
towards those who first come to him. Jesus himself had
already depicted the warmth and joy with which he wel-
comes those who turn to him in the parables of the lost
sheep, the lost coin, and the prodigal son in Luke 15. We
ought to welcome new brothers and sisters into our lives

with the same kind of eagerness and love that Christ has for them.

Evangelism is a much discussed topic these days. Many Christians are trying to find more effective ways to proclaim the good news of Jesus Christ. Yet often an essential element of evangelism is neglected — welcoming a person who becomes interested in the Lord into our lives. Many fail to continue in a Christian life (or in a new Christian life they have begun) because they cannot find a home among Christians. Few of these people can persevere on their own.

The Life in the Spirit Seminars have an evangelistic purpose, but they are primarily designed as instruction. In the seminars, people can make contact with a Christian community, learn about the new life in Christ that they can receive, and be helped in taking the first steps of that life. But this is only a part of what each new person needs. If he does not become part of the life of the community or prayer group at the same time, he will probably not experience much growth in the life of the Spirit. The Life in the Spirit Seminars must be accompanied by a process of "greeting" people.

"Greeting" people simply means welcoming them into our life and helping them become a part of it. It is a type of pastoral-shepherdly-activity. It could be called "pastoral evangelism", because a greeter works with those who are becoming interested in a new life in Christ as a pastor or shepherd: he watches where the new people are, keeps in contact with them and helps them to find their place in the community or prayer group.

"Greeting" happens naturally within a small group of Christians who have learned to love others the way Christ loves them. Such Christians will naturally keep in contact with new people and include them in their life. But when a group of Christians gets to be larger than thirty or forty people, newcomers are no longer so noticeable and so they no longer get welcomed. Some sort of pastoral concern is needed.

One group of people who will often do "greeting" is the team members for the Life in the Spirit Seminars. They are in personal contact with new people from the very beginning. In a small prayer group, those who work on the seminars will often do the greeting, without making a distinction between their work as greeters and their work as team members.

The growth of a community or prayer group will usually create a need for some better means of greeting people. When a large number of people is being added to the community or prayer group and the team members are accumulating a large number of people to greet, something else is needed. Generally, this point comes fairly early in the growth of any prayer group or community.

When the Life in the Spirit Seminars are being given for people who live over a wide geographical area or in a prayer group or community that is large enough to have subgroupings, there is a particular need to have a better way to greet new people. The seminars themselves can be presented centrally without losing any effectiveness, but each new person needs to be connected with a subgrouping or local segment of the community that is located in the area he lives in. The person who greets him must be familiar with the part of the community or prayer group that the new person will be connected with. The greeter is the link between the central seminars and the subgrouping or local situation.

Greeting only works when there is something to welcome new people into. It makes no sense to have a team of greeters if there is not a group of people who have some kind of real commitment to living the life of the Spirit with one another. The purpose of greeting is to connect those who are newly interested in living that life together and who can be a help to the new person.

# THE GREETERS TEAM

The greeters team is the group of people in a community or prayer group (or in a section of the community or prayer group) that cares for the new people until they become joined to the life of that group. When they work together as a team they can be much more effective in helping the new people than when they are working individually. The effective functioning of a greeters team is one of the keys to effective evangelism and growth in numbers for a community or prayer group.

The greeters team can be the same group that puts on the Life in the Spirit Seminars for a community or prayer group, or it can be a separate group. Or there can be a separate greeters team, but it can include some people who also work on Life in the Spirit Seminars. Whatever the particular arrangements, the greeters team or teams should work very closely with those who work on the seminars. Greeting and working in the seminars are two aspects of the same process.

In order for the process of bringing new people into the life of a community or prayer group to function properly, there should be one person, or a small group of people, responsible for the whole area as a "pastor" or "elder". That person should have the authority over the area to see that it develops properly and that people are being well cared for. His main attention should be focused on the whole process of bringing people into the life of the community or prayer group, not just on presenting the Life in the Spirit Seminars as a program.

**The leader of a greeters team** could be either the person who is responsible for the whole process of bringing new people into the life of the community or prayer group, or he could be a person who works under him. His role and the requirements for filling that role are the same as those for the team leader in the seminars (p. 21). Like the team leader, he has a pastoral role, the role of an elder in a Christian community, and he should therefore take a pastoral care for the people who are entering into the community or prayer group.

**The greeters** themselves should meet the same requirements as the members of the seminar team (p. 23). They should work under the direction of the team leader, and come to the greeters meeting each week. They should work as greeters for some time (it often takes a number of months of experience to become effective at greeting), and when they first begin they should work closely under the direction of the team leader or an experienced greeter. When a greeter leaves the team, he should be phased out, and any people whom he is still responsible for should be transferred to another greeter.

**The greeters meeting** should be held weekly. It is a time for both taking care of the practical arrangements of the greeting process and for building the greeters into a strong and effective team. The section "Working together as one" (p. 24) applies to the greeters team as well as to the Life in the Spirit Seminars team. The greeters team meeting should involve the following elements:

— prayer
— sharing about better ways of greeting (this includes sharing about the right attitudes and about the way to approach it spiritually as well as sharing about methods)
— discussion of what is happening with individuals and how to help them
— working out any practical arrangements
— transfer of information between the greeters, the Life in the Spirit Seminar team members, and others in the community or prayer group who have a concern for the new people
— periodic evaluation of how the greeters team or the team meeting is functioning.

# THE WORK OF THE GREETER

**Purpose**

The greeter is responsible for welcoming new people into the life of the community or prayer group and for helping them until they are actively part of that community or prayer group. Specifically he should:

1. connect new people with the ongoing life of the community or prayer group by:
    — encouraging them to regularly attend community meetings
    — inviting them to come to any meetings that are only for community members and seeing that they feel at home
    — introducing them to others in the community, especially to those who can most easily identify with them or who could be of most help to them
    — inviting them to parties, Bible studies, special Eucharists, or any other appropriate community events
    — encouraging them to participate in the program of instruction that follows the Life in the Spirit Seminars;

2. take a brotherly or sisterly concern for the new people by:
    — keeping regular, friendly contact with them
    — encouraging good habits in them (regular prayer, Scripture reading, spiritual reading, etc.)
    — detecting any spiritual problem or any other types of problems that would affect their growth in the Spirit and either helping them with those problems or seeing that they find any help that is available;

3. supplement the work of the Life in the Spirit team
   member by:
   — helping determine where people stand (do they
       have a commitment to Christ, what is their
       relationship to their churches, how are they
       responding to the seminar)
   — finding out any basic information that is not on
       the sign-up cards (church affiliation, family,
       etc.)
   — determining if they have been involved in drug
       use, the occult or eastern religions, or if there
       is need for serious change in their lives before
       they should be prayed with. Specifics of ser-
       ious wrongdoing or criminal action should
       not be written down unless it is public know-
       ledge. At all times we should take care to ap-
       proach this area with the appropriate degree
       of confidentiality.
   — determining whether they are open to receiving
       spiritual gifts, especially tongues.
   (The team member does not always have the kind
       of contact with people that brings out all of
       these things; many problems will not be re-
       vealed by the sharing in the discussion groups.)

The greeter is not a personal counselor. He can sometimes help people with particular problems, but his primary
role is not counseling, but simply connecting people with
the life of the community or prayer group. Often counseling can become so time-consuming that it prevents greeters
from working with many people.

The greeter's responsibility for a particular person
ends when that person is genuinely joined to the life of
the community. If a community or prayer group is well
ordered, the greeter's responsibility will not end until someone else takes up the responsibility for that person's pastoral care.

# METHOD OF GREETING

1) Contact with the new people should be made *as soon as possible;* when the contact can be built into the Life in the Spirit Seminars by having the greeters come and meet the people at the end of the second session, it should be done that way.

2) A private face to face contact with the new people before the fifth week is necessary; other contacts do not have to be lengthy and can be done by telephone.

3) In order to maintain regular contact with the new people (preferably weekly), set aside a definite time with them.

4) If it is possible or practical, invite them to dinner; this is a good way to establish a relationship of love and trust and go beyond a formal relationship.

5) Use other people in the community or prayer group to help in greeting; especially use the people who were their first contact with the community or who were in any way instrumental in helping them begin the seminars.

6) If possible, contact the new people with families, households, or other small groups in the community who could take a responsibility for making them feel welcome.

7) When greeting both husband and wife, it is a good idea to occasionally talk to them separately; preferably they should be greeted by husband and wife greeters.

8) When you cannot take on responsibility for another new person, say so beforehand.

# SOME SUGGESTIONS

1) Pray for the people whom you are greeting; also pray for your fellow greeters and your meetings together.

2) Be persistent; do not be timid; ask the Lord for holy boldness — many people need human encouragement to go on.

3) You may often develop a feeling or sense about a problem area that you cannot easily define or communicate to a Life in the Spirit Seminar team member; if so, share it with other greeters and then discuss it with the person's discussion group leader.

4) You need not center all of your contacts on spiritual things; often casual conversation will reveal a number of ways that you can help a person's spiritual growth.

5) Be prepared to hear lies from Satan or from yourself about your ability to be a greeter or about the importance of greeting; if you feel guilty about any lack of conscientiousness in your greeting work, if you feel inadequate spiritually or any other way in relation to some person you are greeting, just call upon the power of God's Spirit to overcome these feelings; our Lord is always with us when we need him, and he wants us to be where he can use us.

# INFORMATION TRANSFER

An effective system of information transfer is essential if the greeters and the Life in the Spirit Seminar team members are to work together. If all the team members are greeters, the transfer could be done orally at the greeters meeting. Normally however, there will have to be written communication. In order for this to work properly:
— there should be a time at the end of the seminar team meeting for the information transfer sheets to be filled out (this can be marked in the manual)
— there should be a time at the end of the greeters meet-

ing for the information transfer sheets to be filled
out
- there should be someone or some group of people responsible for seeing that the transfer sheets are taken from one group to another
- the information of the sheets should be kept strictly confidential.

If transfer sheets are used, they can be given to the person who has the pastoral responsibility for the new person when the greeter's responsibility ends.

For the comments on the transfer sheets to be effective, they should cover all the basic points and be clear. The person writing the comments should avoid all generalities and vague statements like "doing OK", "Wow", or "having problems". He should clearly state what the person is experiencing, where he is at, and how to encourage him and deal with his problems.

Both the discussion leader and the greeter should fill in any initial basic information such as his background (religious, occupational, living situation), how he first came in contact with the community or prayer group, why he started the seminars, what his present understanding of Christianity is, what noticeable problems he is having. The discussion leader should give weekly feedback on the person's response to each session, on his understanding of the teaching, on his sharing in the discussion group, on problems in faith, prayer, tongues, or any other area the greeter should give encouragement in. The greeter should provide feedback on what he sees of the person's response to the seminar each week, and also information on his own contacts with the person being greeted and the person's involvement and participation in community activities. Both the discussion leader and the greeter should comment specifically between the fourth and fifth weeks about the person's readiness and willingness to change his life and be prayed with, and after the sixth week about the extent to which the person has connected himself with the life of the community or prayer group. If a person drops out of the seminar, either the discussion leader or the greeter should find out why and communicate the reasons to the other.

> "My brothers, if any one among you wanders from the truth and someone brings him back, let him know that whoever brings back a sinner from the error of his way will save his soul from death and will cover a multitude of sins."
>
> (James 5:19-20)